Celtic Christianity and Climate Crisis

Twelve Keys for the Future of the Church

— RAY SIMPSON —

Sacristy Press
PO Box 612, Durham, DH1 9HT

www.sacristy.co.uk

First published in 2020 by Sacristy Press, Durham

Sacristy Limited, registered in England & Wales, number 7565667

British Library Cataloguing-in-Publication Data
A catalogue record for the book is available from the British Library

ISBN 978-1-78959-115-6

Contents

Foreword

It was a little over twenty-five years ago that I wrote a foreword for Ray's first book *Exploring Celtic Christianity*. Since then have flowed an amazing range of published books covering such subjects as Celtic liturgies and daily prayers, biographies and church history, soul friendship and new monasticism.

This signals a simple truth which is that Celtic Christianity has come of age and earned its place as an equal contributor at the table of ecumenical Christian dialogue. Granted that, there has been a catalogue of oversimplifications and too much romanticizing of the image of the so-called Celtic Church. But which expression of church has not had similar parodies and assumptions of its true structure in the course of their development? It is not that long ago that leaders of some of the new church developments heralded their church as being free from the strangulation of years of organizational restriction within established denominations and a return to the unfettered unity of the early Church of the apostolic period. A cursory reading of the book of Acts will explode these seductive myths fairly comprehensively.

In this new book, Ray Simpson tables twelve criticisms of Celtic Christianity. He does in fact describe them as twelve keys of unique insight and resource found corporately within the expression of the Celtic Churches of the British Isles. Such keys are essential rhythms by which community and creation may be renewed. *Celtic Christianity and Climate Crisis* demonstrates the remarkable breadth of Ray's research and scholarship perhaps more than any other book he has written.

Having known Ray for almost thirty years, I am happy to point out that there is another fundamental and important element to be found in this book. Ray lives the issues he proclaims. These are not academic, well-honed theological concepts which could for all intent and purpose be gained by never leaving the library. These are the rhythms of his own faith walk and as such they have been worked on, changed, some discarded but many more refreshed and brought to a new clarity of conviction. These are convictions we can all live by.

Russ Parker
Co-founder of the Community of Aidan and Hilda

Introduction

The systems that dominate our economics, politics and much religion are based on humankind taking more and more from a finite world. The climate crisis reveals the truth expressed by the sixth-century Irish saint Columbanus: "If you trample the earth the earth will trample you."

Unredeemed capitalism has rushed ahead with de-regulation of the corporate sector, privatization of the public sector, and cuts in corporate taxes paid for with cuts to public spending. As Naomi Klein points out in her penetrating book *This Changes Everything*, the heart of our economic model is grow or die.[1] Free world trade has vastly increased exports and imports of fossil fuel-enabled products—much based on greed, none of it based on care for the environment. This is now in conflict with the imperative of the environment crisis: steward or die. We have to come out of denial. A worldview needs to arise that sees nature, other nations and our own neighbours as partners in a grand project of mutual reinvention.

The tragedy is, as Klein's book demonstrates, that religion is seen as one of the forces of denial. The only creation-friendly spirituality that Klein discerns is from First Nations. Many versions, especially of USA evangelical Christianity, use the Genesis 1:28 quote of God saying to humans "subdue the earth . . . have dominion over the creatures" to justify human rape of the earth. This is in fact a distortion of biblical teaching. The world needs to know of a model of creation-friendly Christianity that is free of colonial interpretations. Celtic Christianity offers this. Its time has come for this new era.

My first book, *Exploring Celtic Spirituality: Historic Roots for Our Future*, published by Hodder & Stoughton in 1995, evoked a remarkable response. In 2004, Kevin Mayhew published a revised edition with a study guide which has never been out of print. Verbum in Norway and Boedal in Denmark have published translations with a revised foreword.

In 2014, this was published in the USA as *Celtic Christianity: Deep Roots for a Modern Faith* (Anamchara Books).

After the original publication letters poured in with quotes such as the following:

> I read it twice in two weeks. Throughout most of my adult life (I'm 34 now) I have been searching for something, something I found in your book. As I read each chapter, I felt more and more excited, more and more at home. Here were my own feelings about Christianity put into words.

> I am convinced that this book will nourish faith and vitalize growth points of the coming generation.

> Your book has opened my eyes to the existence of Celtic spirituality, and I find myself intrigued by an approach to the faith that is gentler, more open and more aware of social issues than I have previously experienced . . . Thank you very much for your wonderful book.

> I know that I will be reading it over and over.

> I have been startled at the depth of joy and pain it has evoked!

> I kept asking myself, and God, "What does Celtic monasticism have to say to the twentieth-century Western church?" Reading your book has given me the answer to my question. It puts together many fragments of my life as well as touching my own Celtic roots.

> My heart has been touched in a profound way by your book. It has unearthed a cry that has been in my heart for some years now, but I had not been able to recognize what it was until I read your book.

After years of loss of faith due to the deaths of her twin daughters and now my brother . . . my friend has started to come back to life through the light of Celtic spirituality. What brought her back to faith was reading this book.

I feel that I have to write to you to tell you how much I have learned, enjoyed and been influenced by your book, especially Chapter 21, "One Church". I was stopped in my tracks when I read this chapter. To me it could stand on its own for the impact it had on my own spiritual path. The line "Make your people holy, make your people one" in the prayer at the end of this chapter made my heart sing in the hope that it embodied.

It has given me the answers to many things, and I found it a great inspiration.

I have long been a fan of your books and especially of *Celtic Spirituality*, and I feel sure that it points the way forward to a church in crisis, containing as it does an everyday relevance with deep spiritual values.

After the first edition of this book was published, a Cambridge physicist told me he felt the book was highly significant and provided the Church's agenda for the next thirty years. The person who had given him the book was a prophetess trusted by Pope John Paul I.

Rowan Williams, a Celt who became Archbishop of Canterbury in 2002, added his voice to those who call for a new way of seeing, and challenged Christians to recapture the imagination of the nation.

The international Community of Aidan and Hilda, whose emergence was described in the first chapter of Part One, has worked hard to enable interested readers to develop life-giving rhythms and the disciplines of a way of life. It now provides resources from The Open Gate Retreat House on the Holy Island of Lindisfarne and through websites such as <https://www.aidanandhilda.org.uk>.

Over the following years, interest has mushroomed in Celtic spirituality of diverse kinds, both Christian and pagan. Some of this

Celtic spirituality has brought renewal; some of it has been divorced from historical roots, and some publishers have used the Celtic label in ways which no academic would countenance. This has inevitably drawn criticism.

These criticisms range from the serious to the silly. Critics include traditionalists who dislike change; rationalists who dislike imagination; Fundamentalist Bible Christians who assume that "Celtic" means "pagan"; ethnic purists who think that only those who speak a Celtic language can contribute anything authentic; Augustinians who dismiss today's creation-loving Celts as untrue to the tradition; English church lovers who think that the word "Anglo-Saxon" should never be mixed with the word "Celtic" to describe their birth right; historians who can't accept that contemporary religious phenomenology might be as valid a discipline as theirs; academics who dislike inexact use of terms and unsubstantiated claims; and new monastics who feel that Facebook Celtic nostalgias, for example fairy stories and ephemeral art, cheapen their calling.

Since my revised edition I have collected every serious criticism levelled at the concept of Celtic Christianity that I am aware of. I have wrestled with these criticisms and tried to sift the wheat from the weeds. This book examines such criticisms and seeks to learn from them in the light of Christianity's evolution in the third millennium. It then explores some soundly based developments in Celtic Christianity that are keys that can unlock possibilities in a new era.

CHAPTER 1

God is at the heart of creation calling us to heal it

In his article "The End of Celtic Christianity", Gilbert Markus writes:

> One of the central planks of romantic Celtic Christian mythology
> is its supposedly distinctive attitude to the natural world. But
> the view of happy Celts living in perfect harmony with nature is
> totally unrealistic. They were constantly praying for protection
> from nature which was deeply threatening.[2]

Markus quotes in evidence the ninth-century prayer of St Sanctan: "May Christ save us from bloody death, from fire, from raging sea . . . may the Lord each hour come to me against wind, against swift waters."

Gilbert Markus and Thomas Owen Clancy recycle the assumption that poems contained in selections such as Jackson's *Celtic Nature Poetry* are untypical poems written by armchair hangers-on, and that poems from the Iona tradition are Augustinian in their views.[3]

Ian Bradley states that in his earlier books *The Celtic Way* and *Is God Green?* he presented Celtic Christianity as eco-friendly and affirmative of the natural world, but that he has substantially changed his view.[4]

The danger of being over-simplistic affects writers on both sides of this argument. It is not disputed that much nature poetry has come down to us from the early Christian centuries in Ireland and Britain. K. H. Jackson's two books *Studies in Early Celtic Nature Poetry* and *A Celtic Miscellany*, and Mary Low's *Celtic Christianity and Nature: Early Irish and Hebridean Traditions* furnish us with much material.[5] Some writers claim, however, that there is little that is distinctive about early Celtic nature poetry, since most ancient societies were close to nature. There is evidence, however, of a Christian theology of God in nature from the earliest period of the Church in Celtic lands onwards.

Pelagius wrote in the fourth century to one of his spiritual directees:

> Look at the animals roaming the forest: God's spirit dwells within them. Look at the birds flying across the sky: God's spirit dwells within them. Look at the tiny insects crawling in the grass: God's spirit dwells within them. Look at the fish in the river and sea ... There is no creature on earth in whom God is absent ... his breath had brought every creature to life ... God's spirit is present within plants as well. The presence of God's spirit in all living things is what makes them beautiful; and if we look with God's eyes, nothing on earth is ugly.[6]

Early Celtic commentators stress that one reason why the creation came into being was that the character of God might be learned through a study of it; see, for example, St Patrick's *Tripartite Life* 1:115: "Not less does the disposition of the elements set forth concerning God and manifest Him than though it were a teacher who set forth and preached it with his lips."

Columbanus, the sixth-century Irish missionary monk, probably had more influence in Europe than any other contemporary Irish person, through his popular faith communities. He taught his followers (see the first of his Collected Sermons): "If you would know the Creator, get to know his creation" and "if you trample on the earth the earth will trample on you."

In a letter to Pope Gregory often attributed to him, he opposes Rome's proposed new computation for deciding the date of Easter on the grounds that creation has a voice: the length of light must exceed the length of darkness:

> And if the moon has begun to shine in the third watch, there is no doubt that the twenty-first or twenty-second moon has arisen, on which it is impossible for the true Easter to be offered. For those who determine that Easter can be celebrated at this period of the moon, not only cannot maintain this on the authority of holy

scripture, but also incur the charge of sacrilege and contumacy, together with the peril of their souls, when they maintain that the true light, which rules over all darkness, can be offered under conditions where darkness rules to some extent.[7]

The seventh-century "Irish Augustine"—an unnamed theologian so-called because he was thought to echo the theological framework of Augustine of Hippo—clearly believed in a three-decker universe—heaven, earth, hell. The Irish Augustine reads the Bible on the assumption "that all of God's acts . . . must have been accomplished in accordance with nature and not in contravention of its laws". According to John Carey in *A Single Ray of the Sun*:

> For Augustinus Hibernicus, God and God's actions are everywhere in the world around us: nature is a manifestation of the heavenly mind and will. His science was a sacred science: to explain all of the wonders of faith in the light of reason and nature was for him an act of homage, not defiance, to the Almighty. The spot where Augustinus knelt to worship became a battleground in the Renaissance; and the war between Science and Religion has raged, often to the detriment of both, down to the present day. One would be hard-pressed to find another Christian writer of any age (or, indeed, of any of the major Western faiths) who so forcefully rejected dualism. For Augustinus, miracles were not contrary to nature; all of nature was miraculous. The world was shot through and through with wonder; every bush and stone was a source of awe.[8]

Augustinus was reaching for a way of relating to the world that does not separate mind and heart. And this too was a corollary of his unitary theology: "We are only able to perceive in part even the bodily things which we see," he wrote. We are not omniscient and face mystery on every side.

In an ancient Irish story of the creation of Adam, which survived as part of "imaginative re-workings and complementary additions to the canon" of scripture, Adam is made, not just of the dust of the earth, but of seven different elements of creation: earth, sea, sun, clouds, wind, stones and light.[9] Different aspects of the whole of creation are interwoven with us.

Creation-friendly attitudes are displayed in the lives and legends of innumerable saints of early Egypt, Ireland and Britain. Helen Waddell's *Beasts and Saints* contains many of these stories. The story of Kevin, the sixth-century hermit of the two-lake valley of Glendalough, where Ireland's Wicklow Mountains meet, offers multiple insights into a Celtic attitude to nature.[10]

Kevin's mother took him to the Fort of the White Fountain, where cattle and wild animals came to find grass, and wise women helped to foster him. After training as a monk, he withdrew to a place of solitude near the Upper Lake at Glendalough. His clothes were the skins of wild animals, his bed a sheet of rock, and his pillow a stone. Each day he stood up to his waist in the lake chanting psalms and prayers, taming some wild creature that curled itself around him. Then he would scramble up to a cave fifty feet above the lake for long vigils of prayer and sleep. According to his legendary *Life*, the leaves of the trees sang sweet songs when he prayed, and he said that "all the wild creatures on the mountains are my house-mates, gentle and familiar with me". Each Lent Kevin would keep vigil in a wattled hut. There he lay on the flagstone with his arms stretched out in the shape of his saviour's cross, and with the palms of his hands open to heaven. So long and still did he lie there that a blackbird made the hollow of his hand its nest and laid an egg. It was said that gentle Kevin, steely of will, stayed thus until the egg was hatched. Although this hagiography is late and legendary, it tells us things about the mind-set of those who told and wrote the stories.

There are stories of Celtic saints who gave sanctuary to animals that others hunted. These include Cadoc, whose protection of a deer and grace towards the hunters brought conversion to Illtud, who later established a learning community in which agriculture was part of the learning, and Melangell, who protected a hare at Pennant Melangell. Stories like these mesh with a repeated theme in the Bible: when people went into deserted places, they encountered God and drew close to the animals.

A British catechism (probably eighth century, but sometimes attributed to St Ninian) goes like this:

What is best in this world?

A: To do the will of our Maker.

What is his will?

A: That we should live according to the laws of his creation.

How do we know those laws?

A: By study ...

And what is the fruit of study?

A: To perceive the eternal Word of God reflected
in every plant and insect, every bird and
animal, and every man and woman.

We know that the Columba family of churches resonated strongly with the Johannine tradition. Bede's account of the case put forward by the Iona monks at Northumbria's Synod of Whitby makes clear that they drew their inspiration from all the teachings of John to the churches in the East. John's teaching that all creation comes forth from The Word—the Second Person of the Trinity—flowered in the poetry of the Northumbrians, who themselves were the flower of the Irish Mission brought by Columba's monks to the English in the seventh century.

The *Life of Cuthbert* by an anonymous monk of Lindisfarne, then by Bede and then the hermit Guthlac's hagiographer Felix, all tell of hermits who enjoyed a special relationship with the elements, birds and animals. Nick Mayhew-Smith[11] suggests it was this relationship with nature that led Bede to write his theological formula about our "lost dominion" over creation. Bede writes in his *Life* of Cuthbert: "For if a man faithfully and wholeheartedly serves the maker of all created things, it is no wonder that all creation should minister to his commands and wishes." He also points out that Bishop Germanus reported a church that met under leafy trees, and that in contrast to missionaries on the Continent who chopped down trees at pagan shrines, there is no hint that any Celtic missionaries did this—indeed they cherished trees. Adomnan mentions that worshippers only went indoors at the point the bread and wine were received—the assumption is that much worship took place outdoors, a practice which Forest Church in our day seeks to re-establish.

Felix added two of his own reasons why nature rituals were important: because a true Christian is united with every other creature in communion with God and because this is a way to meet with the angels. His exact words are: "Have you not read that if a man is joined to God in purity of spirit, all things are united to him in God? He who refuses to be acknowledged by men seeks the recognition of wild beasts . . . he who receives frequent visits from men can not often be visited by angels." Felix traces the latter to a naked hermit of Mount Sinai. Sulpicius Severus, who wrote the *Life of Martin of Tours*, writes about him and other Egyptian hermits in the first volume of his *Dialogues*.

Nick Mayhew-Smith argues persuasively that the vision of the early Celtic Church was to restore communion with creation, which they often picture as restoring Eden. The mythical voyages in the Brendan genre were often to discover an Eden or paradise where the original blessed creation could be re-instituted. Athanasius taught that when Christ immersed himself in the River Jordan, he was inaugurating a new creation by re-uniting it, as well as all humanity, with God. Mayhew-Smith links the Celtic practice of open-air baptisms and regular prayer while submerged in water as a spiritual practice that helped to restore this communion of our bodies and souls with God in creation. This concept was taught by St John Chrysostom: he rejects the idea that baptism is merely about the remission of a person's sins; rather, it is a bodily re-creation, akin to the making of Adam out of earth. Mayhew-Smith links the story of Germanus calming the seas by sprinkling oil on them, with Columba's calming of Loch Ness and its monster and Aidan telling the future queen's escort to sprinkle blessed oil on the troubled waters, with a redeeming of creation, and he quotes a poem, *In Praise of Columcille*, which says: "It was not on soft beds he undertook elaborate prayers, he crucified—it was not for crimes—his body on the green waves."

Cuthbert's actions frequently ended up having a participatory effect on the environment. After he prayed all night in the sea at Coldingham, creation is so moved that it sends two otters to warm his feet. On Epiphany, while evangelizing among the Picts, St Cuthbert's party is stranded upon the shore by a storm, but the sea casts up provisions in the form of dolphin meat that tastes like honey. In the Teviot Hills, Cuthbert prophesies to a boy he is mentoring that an eagle they see flying overhead will bring their meal. It duly deposits a fish, but Cuthbert tells

his companion to give some of the fish to the bird, because he interprets
the bird's behaviour as "fasting".

Perhaps the supreme example of the poetry of Northumbria inspired
by the Irish Mission is *The Dream of the Rood*. Here are extracts from
Elaine Treharne's translation in the *Old and Middle English Anthology*
(Blackwell):

> It seemed to me that I saw a more wonderful tree
> lifted in the air, wound round with light,
> the brightest of beams. That beacon was entirely
> cased in gold; beautiful gems stood
> at the corners of the earth, likewise there were five
> upon the cross-beam. All those fair through creation
> gazed on the angel of the Lord there. There was certainly no
> gallows of the wicked;
> but the holy spirits beheld it there,
> men over the earth and all this glorious creation.
> Yet as I lay there a long while
> I beheld sorrowful the tree of the Saviour,
> until I heard it utter a sound;
> it began to speak words, the best of wood:
> "That was very long ago, I remember it still,
> that I was cut down from the edge of the wood,
> ripped up by my roots. They seized me there, strong enemies,
> made me a spectacle for themselves there, commanded me to
> raise up their criminals.
> Men carried me there on their shoulders, until they set me
> on a hill,
> enemies enough fastened me there. I saw then the Saviour of
> mankind
> hasten with great zeal, as if he wanted to climb up on me . . .
> He stripped himself then, young hero—that
>   was God almighty—
> strong and resolute; he ascended on the high gallows,
> brave in the sight of many, when he wanted to ransom
> mankind.

I trembled when the warrior embraced me; even then I did not
dare to bow to earth,
fall to the corners of the earth, but I had to stand fast.
Darkness had
covered with clouds the Ruler's corpse,
the gleaming light. Shadows went forth
dark under the clouds. All creation wept . . .

John Scotus Eriugena, who was born in Ireland in 815 and educated there
before becoming a famed theologian on the Continent, also reflected the
Johannine creation theology. He is the most significant Irish intellectual
of the early monastic period. He is generally recognized to be both the
outstanding philosopher (in terms of originality) of the Carolingian era
and of the whole period of Latin philosophy stretching from Boethius
to Anselm.

His supreme work, *The Division of Nature*, synthesizes the philosophical
accomplishments of fifteen centuries and is seen by many as the final
achievement of ancient philosophy. In this work, and even more in his
commentary on the prologue to St John's Gospel, he portrays the entire
creation coming from a single point in the heart of The Word (Christ).

Eriugena had a unique gift for identifying the underlying intellectual
framework, broadly Neoplatonic but also deeply Christian, assumed by
the writers of the Christian East. Drawing especially on Basil, Gregory of
Nyssa, Pseudo-Dionysius the Areopagite and Maximus the Confessor, as
well as on the more familiar authorities of the Latin West, he developed
a highly original cosmology, where the highest principle, the immovable
self-identical, engenders all things and retrieves them back into itself.

Eriugena developed a Neoplatonic cosmology, according to which the
infinite God proceeds from his divine "darkness" into the light of being,
speaking the Word who is understood as Christ, and at the same timeless
moment bringing forth the Primary Causes of all creation. These causes in
turn proceed into their Created Effects and as such are creatures entirely
dependent on, and will ultimately return to, their sources, which are the
Causes or Ideas in God. These causes are actually one single principle
in the divine One. The whole of reality or nature, then, is involved in a
dynamic process of outgoing (*exitus*) from and return (*reditus*) to the

One. In this book he explores four forms of creativity: God as originator, causation, matter, and God as the Completer of all. For him all creatures, visible and invisible, are an appearance of God (theophany).

In the early Roman or Latin tradition of evangelization, converts were typically commanded to leave their farmsteads and come inside to a church building. The Irish and British approach, partly inspired by the Egyptian desert fathers and mothers, was to go from the indoors into the outdoors in order to seek God in desert places where they could encounter him in the silence, the wildness and the elements. They had three seasons of Lent, including one for the forty days after Pentecost when the weather encouraged this kind of outdoors approach.

We know that the early Celtic Christians felt a rapport with the Christians of the deserts and of the Eastern churches established by John the Beloved Disciple. We only know the titles of some of the books from those sources that were in their monastic libraries. It is possible that they knew of the teaching of Maximus the Confessor (d. 662) that the Creator-Logos has implanted in each created thing a characteristic "thought" which is God's presence in and intention for it, and which draws it towards God, and that by virtue of this indwelling logos each created thing is not just an object but a personal word addressed to us by the Creator.

There is an abundance of Celtic nature poetry, as Kenneth Jackson's *Studies in Celtic Nature Poetry* attests. This reveals the writers to be keen observers of the natural world, affectionate towards it and celebrating it in poetry and prayer. It seems these are the earliest nature poems in Europe to be written in a mother tongue. The suggestion some have made that these are but the musings of comfortable people far removed from real nature cannot, I think, be sustained.

The Celtic high crosses feature a circle as well as the cross. There are diverse theories as to the origin and meaning of the circle. A leading contender is that the circle represents the sun, and that Christ transforms all that the sun represents. Others expand the meaning of the circle to embrace all creation. Jung understood the circle to be a primal symbol of wholeness.

Most high Celtic crosses include biblical scenes, some of which have animals. The Bewcastle Cross on the English side of the border with Scotland not only has intertwining leaf patterns; it portrays Christ standing on the eagerly raised heads of two "anonymous" and silent animals. Robert Brown suggests their outer paws are raised in the liturgical orans position—a eucharistic acclamation of prayer:[12]

> So it is the pair of anonymous animals, present in heaven, that in their eager silence, lifting their heads while inclining towards each other in an act of fellowship and unity, both proclaim Jesus as the Christ (with their inner paws), and worship him as Lord (with their outer ones). This is a remarkably different depiction from "the writhing creatures that occur elsewhere in Early Christian and early medieval art under the feet of the victorious Christ".

Professor Rosemary Cramp says this "happy relationship between God and the beasts is remarked upon by Bede and can be seen as a hallmark of Celtic saints such as Kentigern, or of his Northumbrian successors such as St Cuthbert".[13] It is notably present also in the eighth-century *Life of Guthlac*. Contrast this with the conflict between man and beast as portrayed, for example, in *Beowulf*.

Zoomorphic art depicts humans or gods as animals often in kaleidoscopic patterns or interspersing with the main figure on a page. This is a characteristic of *The Lindisfarne Gospels* (adopted from Germanic art) which makes extensive use of interlaced animal and bird patterns throughout the book. The birds that appear in the manuscript may also reflect Eadfrith the scribe's observations of wildlife in Lindisfarne:

> The new style of animal ornament that reached a creative peak in the Lindisfarne Gospels therefore exerted considerable influence upon the sculpture and metalwork of eighth century northern Britain and Ireland . . . The animal interlace . . . is combined with a swirling vortex of abstract spiral work and curvilinear trumpet and pelta forms derived from Celtic La Tene art. The movement implicit in these designs is reminiscent of the flow of water and air and the burgeoning of plant life . . . An analogy with the creatures and forces of Earth, Air and Water in Genesis 1 is suggested.[14]

Winding or interlaced vines are commonly seen on high crosses, tapestries, writings, knot work, and Gospel manuscripts. Scholars doubt whether we can know their original meaning. Some meanings commonly read into them are life, diversity, regeneration, continuity, fertility, bounty, growth and interconnections with eternity. Jesus often used vines as illustrations of fruitful relationship: "I am the Vine and my Father is the vine grower . . . you are branches. If you abide in me and I abide in you, you will bring forth much fruit" (John 15:1, 4). The prophet Isaiah and Jesus liken planet earth to a vineyard that God calls us to tend.

The Carmina Gadelica, or *Songs of the Gael*, Alexander Carmichael's late nineteenth-century collections of prayers and poems, remembered and orally handed down in the homes of Scotland's Gaelic-speaking western isles, is indeed far removed from the Celtic-speaking churches of the first millennium. Three influences can be clearly detected in the poems and sayings: the Roman Catholic (especially in an island such as Harris), the Reformed Presbyterian (especially in an island such as Lewis) and general folklore which blends pagan with nominal Christian mind-sets. Yet among this vast collection some poems stand out as a love affair with God in his creation, such as the following:

There's no plant in the ground
But is full of his blessing
There's no thing in the sea
But is full of his life
There is nought in the sky
But proclaims his goodness
Jesu! O Jesu! it's good to praise thee!
There's no bird on the wing
But is full of his blessing
There's no star in the sky
But is full of his life
There is nought neath the sun
But proclaims his goodness
Jesu! O Jesu! it's good to praise thee!

Carmina Gadelica

The accusation that Celts found nature threatening and did not view creation through rose-tinted spectacles seems to me to be evidence that they were realistic. However, whereas in the myths of the Vikings the gods were vengeful, in the Celtic tradition God could be angry but not capricious. Aidan's disciple Chad, a Saxon schooled in the Irish tradition, used to stop what he was doing and lie prostrate when there was a thunderstorm. He quoted Psalm 18 and took it to be God's stern voice thundering so we would plead with God for mercy upon humankind.

Aidan urged Abbot Utta, the leader of the escort for the Kent bride-to-be of King Oswy, to throw a phial of blessed oil on the troubled waters when a storm erupted. This prayer made tangible through anointed oil brought calm to troubled waters. These Celts did not take lightly the harshness of nature, but they sought God even in the harsh elements.

There are over 2,500 references to the land in the Old Testament and 250 in the New Testament. Celtic popularists often claim that in Celtic spirituality people, place and God come together.

Young people rise up across the world calling us to save the planet from extinction. They point to runaway climate chaos and inaction by governments who are in hock to commercial interests. They may have lost faith in politicians, but need they lose faith in God?

Churches reflected in their theologies the pride that humans are over and above the rest of creation. It is widely believed that a trio of scientists—Copernicus, Darwin and Freud—inflicted three irreparable wounds on humanity's pride. The beliefs that this earth is the centre of importance, that humans are distinct from the animals, and that the soul can be separated from our animal conditioning are now seen to be illusions. Where does that leave God, the Bible and religion? Fundamentalists close their minds to these three realities—partial though they are. They become keen Christians with shrill voices who fail to win the most thoughtful people.

In contrast, Celtic Christianity accepts the truth that the world is round, but still finds God in the circlings of light and of life. It accepts that we are all part of one groaning, evolving creation, but it finds the Cosmic Birther accompanying the groaning creation from within. It accepts the truth that humans share animal DNA but refuses to close its mind to the possibility that the human journey leads upwards to ever greater glories.

That is not how Christianity is generally perceived, however. More than fifty years ago, *Science* magazine published *The Historical Roots of our Ecologic Crisis* (March 1967). The paper by Lynn White, then Professor of History at the University of California, argued that the Judaeo-Christian religion was at the root of our ecologic crisis. He argued that the Genesis creation narratives give humankind license to be masters of all creatures. This inculcated the notion that humans are distinct from and above the rest of nature, and that nature exists in order to meet human needs. This left humans free to plunder and control natural resources as they wished.

White went further. He suggested that by destroying pagan approaches to nature Christianity "legitimized the exploitation of Nature in a mood of indifference to the feelings of natural objects". He argued that this dogma gave science and technology powers which, to judge by many of the ecologic effects, are out of control. He concluded, "if so, Christianity bears a huge burden of guilt."

White did not address the problem of how we build the architecture of civilized values if we throw out all religion. Celtic spirituality, like Orthodox spirituality, has never lost the sense of the unity of all creation in the praise of God, as A. M. Allchin draws out in his anthology of Welsh poetry *Praise Above All: Discovering the Welsh Tradition*.

The sense of an intuitive and intimate link between the creation and the Creator went deep into the soul, not only of the Irish, but of the Anglo-Saxons who were formed in the Irish tradition of St Aidan. As we have seen, that epic Northumbrian poem, *The Dream of the Rood*, in which the tree on which Jesus was crucified speaks, interpreting the Gospel accounts of earthquakes and sun's eclipse when the Son of God was killed upon the cross, sums up this cosmic tragedy in the immortal phrase "all creation wept". Redemption and creation become one in the image of the Tree of Death that becomes the Tree of Life.

The divorce between creation and the Creator, and between human life and creation, which took place in many parts of Europe during the ages of Rationalism and Industrialism, has not taken place in Celtic spirituality.

This understanding of Christ in creation is absent from a majority of families who shop in supermarkets. Persistent stories circulate that when schoolchildren are asked where milk comes from, they reply "the supermarket". They have no knowledge of a cow. Christian discipleship courses collude with this diseased education. Introductory courses to Christianity, such as the Alpha course, often lack a unit on Christ in Creation.

The world faces environmental catastrophe unless unprecedented measures are taken to curb global warming. That warning was issued in October 2018 by the United Nations' Inter-Governmental Panel on Climate Change (IPCC). Planet earth stares ecological disaster in the face. The evidence from the IPCC and a phalanx of other scientists is overwhelming. In his book *The Uninhabitable Earth*, David Wallace-Wells foretells in each of the twelve chapters a specific disaster if the world does not wake up to the damage it is inflicting; for example, heat death, dying oceans, unbreathable air, plagues of warming.[15]

The world's great religions must step up to this challenge, yet many people who care about the environment perceive the Christian Church to be an agent of the belittlement of creation, giving it no spirit and value other than its utility to human beings. The Norwegian founder of deep ecology, Arne Naess, was convinced that spiritualities that linked the sacredness of the soul and the sacredness of creation were intrinsic to ecology, but that the Judaeo-Christian tradition was like a cancer on the biosphere because it arrogantly thought that humans had a divine mandate to dominate creation.

Christians can argue, as I do, that this is a misreading of Scripture, which consistently teaches that creation is an expression of God. We cannot, however, deny that this perception of Christianity as anti-ecological is widespread, nor that both Roman and Reformed churches are guilty of some of the accusations levelled at them. So, to bring an expression of Christianity that *is* creation-friendly out of the cellar and into the front room is both important and timely.

Commenting on the prologue to John's Gospel, Philip Newell, a former warden at Iona Abbey, observes in his book *Christ of the Celts* that "John is listening to the universe as an expression of God. It is spoken into being by the One from whom all things come. It comes directly from the heart of God's being. And in it we can hear the sound of the one Heartbeat. The whiteness of the moon, the wildness of the wind, the moisture of the fecund earth is the glow and whiteness and moistness of God now."[16]

David Adam concludes his magnificent book *Love the World* with words such as these: "I am the quantum expanding forth . . . I am the aeons of time . . . I am No-Thing yet I fill all things, I am who I am."[17]

One modern Celtic Christian community which does this is the Society of St Columba, led by Greg Valerio MBE. They describe themselves as "a diverse group consisting of Anglicans, Copts, Evangelicals, non-conformists and individuals whose faith journey would not really know what any of these words mean". Greg Valerio writes in their blog:

> In 2016 Larry and Deborah Littlebird visited us from New Mexico and spoke to us about starting all over again. This had a profound impact on many of us. If the life affirming message of Jesus Christ is to systemically take root once again in the British Isles, we must not assume we know what this means. The aggressive secular socio-political challenges that Britain and our wider western world face will not be resolved through a business as usual ecclesiastical approach to churchmanship and economics. We sense there is a wisdom in the slower more agrarian sustainable ecclesiology as practised by the Celtic Monastic Church and exemplified by St. Columba. Hence our call to join us in establishing this most ancient of ways in a contemporary setting.

He continues:

> We feel called to get our hands dirty and build from the ground up, literally. To plant, to care for creation, to rebuild and repurpose the ancient landscape. To dig out old wells and drink from them, to walk together in pilgrimage, to pray and listen together and to learn from one another under the guidance of the Holy Spirit. At Great Farm in Chanctonbury, these words are not prophetic platitudes, conceptual spiritual ideals that fit nicely in with existing comfort-filled lifestyles. These are actual physical manifestations in the land of what God is speaking in three dimensions. We will plant a market garden, orchard, vineyard, tend our livestock, re-establish the old well, renovate buildings, prepare food for people and establish a library and learning

centre. These tasks speak of starting over, establishing a rhythm of heaven on earth and a table of hospitality where everyone is welcome to come and eat. This is not a short-term project, this is an ongoing work that will always be in development, as it is heavenly community formation.[18]

Celtic Christianity must become mainstream. The world needs to draw inspiration from people who cherish creation because they find God at its heart.

CHAPTER 2

Indigenous principles of mission are more important than surface uniformity

Catherine Thom claims that the Synod of Whitby marks the suppression of the Celtic Church by Rome.[19] That popular view is echoed by Celtic Springs, a monthly Fresh Expression that meets at the ancient Saxon Anglican Church at Escomb, County Durham, which used this Lament for the Synod of Whitby at its first service for un-churched people:

The leaders in the Church gathered at Whitby in 664:

Arise O Celtic holy women
Celtic voices spoke for the mountains and
 the islands and the people:
Arise O Celtic holy men
But the power of the continental Church turned the others:
Arise O Celtic holy women
And so the synod pledged the land to the Holy Roman Empire:
Arise O Celtic holy men
The Celtic ways were soon called wrong
 and primitive and dark:
Arise O Celtic holy women
All the Celtic beauty was pushed to the margins:
Arise O Celtic holy men
But the springs of the Spirit of the land
 remained under the ground:
Arise O Celtic holy women

In our days the Empire is dying and the
    Celtic springs flow stronger:
Arise O Celtic holy men
May we take up the vision of the Celtic
    founders of this holy place:
Arise O Celtic holy women
May the healing rivers of the gentle Spirit
    return to our barren land:
Arise O Celtic holy women and men

Father and Mother God, use us to restore true care of the land,
in simple living. Mother and Father God, use us to restore
true honouring of the beauty of the changing seasons and the
myriad creatures. Father and Mother God, use us to restore true
honouring of the springs of the Spirit. Mother and Father God,
use us to restore true love between people and creatures, a love
that cradles the best life for all.[20]

In recent years, a glut of independent "Celtic" churches have proliferated,
mainly in the USA. Some of these come under the umbrella of The Celtic
Christian Communion. This claims to be a coalition of Spirit-filled
churches, including The Ecumenical Order of St Columba, which operate
"in accordance with the teaching of our Lord Jesus Christ as found in
scripture and in the practice and polity of the Christian Faith within the
Celtic lands of the British Isles, and parts of Europe prior to the Synod
of Whitby of 664 AD".

Others argue that the influence of the Synod of Whitby has been
grossly inflated: it affected just one Anglo-Saxon kingdom, and its central
decision, to unify the date of Easter, was no more than common sense. A
Roman Catholic bishop assured me that it merely "preserved the links"
between the Church in England and in the rest of the Christian world.

Benedicta Ward argues that the Synod of Whitby was "in no way
an anti-Irish, pro-Roman tussle. That was the view of churchmen in
the nineteenth century who were concerned with their own problems
about English-Roman church differences, and not of seventh-century
Northumbria. It is a misconception which is now creating the fantasy of a

'Celtic Spirituality.'" Her cavalier and sour footnote 133 adds: "Bookshops now stock shelves full of books on 'Celtic Spirituality', many of which have nothing either Celtic or spiritual about them."[21]

Where does the truth lie?

In 664 Oswy, ruler of the Saxon kingdom of Northumbria, called a church synod at Whitby to determine whether Northumbria's churches should keep Easter on the date observed by Iona and the Columban family of churches in Ireland whose mission had established churches in Northumbria, or on the date prescribed by Rome; and to determine whether monks should have the tonsure prescribed by Rome or that worn among churches in Ireland and Britain, which allowed long hair at the back of the head, and to introduce many smaller Roman regulations. As a result, all the Irish monks and thirty Saxon monks at Lindisfarne returned to Ireland. The Irish established their new monastery on the island of Inishbofin, and the Saxons established theirs at Mayo.

It is certainly true that the synod did not end Irish influence among the English. Saxons discipled by Aidan became missionary bishops; for example, Chad in Mercia and Cedd among the East Saxons. In the late seventh century, a southern Irish monk named Maildubh established a hermitage at Malmesbury where the local children were taught. Towards the end of his life the area was conquered by the Saxons. Around 676, one of his pupils, the scholar-poet Aldhelm, was appointed abbot. He re-ordered the hermitage as a Benedictine monastery and the town of Malmesbury grew around the expanding abbey.

After Oswy died in 670 and his successor, Ecgfrith, was killed while fighting the Irish and Picts, the Northumbrian succession fell to Aldfrith. He was the son of Oswy's liaison with an Irish princess of the Uí Niall dynasty, probably Fín. He was a friend of Iona's abbot Adomnan and may well have studied at Durrow with him. Bede's *Life of Cuthbert* recounts a conversation between Cuthbert and Abbess Ælfflæd of Whitby, daughter of Oswy, in which Cuthbert foresaw Ecgfrith's death and she asked about his successor: "She therefore understood him to speak of [Aldfrith], who was said to be the son of her father, and was then, on account of his love of literature, exiled to the Scottish islands." St Cuthbert was a second cousin of Aldfrith according to some Irish genealogies. Aldfrith oversaw the creation of works of Hiberno-Saxon art such as the Lindisfarne Gospels and the Codex Amiatinus, and is often seen as the start of Northumbria's golden age.

The rules agreed by the Synod of Whitby affected only the Saxon kingdom of Northumbria. Other kingdoms or monastic families in southern Ireland had already accepted the Roman date for Easter before 664, and other kingdoms in Britain and Ireland accepted it at various later dates over a considerable period of time: North of Ireland in 692, Wessex, East Devon and Somerset in 705, the Picts in 710, Iona 716–18, Strathclyde 721, North Wales 768, parts of Cornwall 909.

The decision to follow the Roman monastic tonsure and date of Easter, and the decision of Lindisfarne's Irish monks and thirty of its Saxon monks to emigrate to Ireland rather than accept the new ways, did not indicate that from that date churches were either Roman or independent. All the churches involved continued to think of themselves as part of the one, apostolic and catholic church. The Lindisfarne monks returned to Ireland as part of St Columba's family of churches which had never had to accept the "new" date of Easter. Later, they did accept it. Strictly speaking, the term Roman Catholic only became normative at the time of the Council of Trent (1564).

At the time the universal church was evolving, issues such as the date of Easter were matters for discussion. Thus, in the 630s, Pope Honorius I sent a letter to Cummian, who was in the south of Ireland and perhaps Abbot of Durrow, about the date of Easter. Cummian took a year to study the question and then called a conference of church elders to consider the matter.

Northumbria was, however, the largest and most significant of the English kingdoms, and the synod was about much more than the date of Easter, so it is perhaps fair to give it an iconic role.

In the longer term, I think a common date for Easter in Western Christendom was almost inevitable—but hairstyles? The Irish monks cut off their hair in a line from ear to ear: the hair at the back of their head flowed long. St Aidan had brought the mission to the Northumbrians in 635 with a commitment not to impose on them the cultural externals of the Iona monks. He believed in planting an indigenous church. Although the Synod of Whitby was only one in a series of Roman impositions, it marked the end of indigenous principles of mission among the

English-speaking peoples. The issue of forcing children of indigenous tribes who had been forcibly placed in colonial schools to cut off their long hair is now considered to be part of the colonial abuse.

Although Bede gives no details of other matters, it is clear from his accounts of Cuthbert when he became Prior of Lindisfarne after the synod, that monks who remained there objected to all kinds of new regulations that came in the wake of the synod. The fact that all the Irish and thirty of the English monks emigrated to Ireland in order to continue their monastic life in their accustomed way suggests that a way of life, a way of relating, a spirituality, was at stake.

H. J. Massingham made this point about the Synod of Whitby: "If the British Church had survived it is possible that the fissure between Christianity and nature, widening through the centuries, would not have cracked the unity of Western man's attitude to the universe."[22]

The failure of Western churches to work with the grain of indigenous peoples is a sin that cries out to heaven. This is illustrated in Euro-American missions to American native peoples. The last of the great Sioux chiefs died in the battle at Wounded Knee, Pine Ridge, at Christmas 1890. Black Elk surveyed the scene and said: "A people's dream died there. There is no center any longer, and the sacred tree is dead."[23]

The late Richard Twiss, a Sicangu Lakota, describes in his two compelling books how the "Christian" cowboys made land possession and money their gods.[24] Their first mistake was that they did not look for signs of the Creator in the tribes. The second mistake was that they told indigenous converts that in order to follow Jesus they had to accept the missionaries' culture and throw away their culture as rubbish. The truth was that the missionaries needed to repent for the rubbish in their own culture, discern what was of God in indigenous culture, and journey with the tribe's Jesus welcomers, asking Jesus to reveal himself in their ceremonies, music, art, dance, customs and aspirations, and to journey together with Jesus to heal the bad things in both First Nation and Western cultures.

From this marginalized position, native peoples have a unique "bias from the bottom" that we would do well to pay attention to. We could learn from them, among other things, that land cannot be owned and Spirit cannot be divided. The earth and all its inhabitants belong to the

Creator who made them. We are called to live in harmony with each other and all created things. Creating harmony is a central idea in most indigenous religions.

Mark Charles (Navajo) is one of many Native Americans who decries "The Doctrine of Discovery" contained in a series of papal bulls (official edicts) written in the fifteenth century. The papal bull *Inter caetera*, issued by Pope Alexander VI on 4 May 1493, played a central role in the Spanish conquest of the New World. The document supported Spain's strategy to ensure its exclusive right to the lands discovered by Columbus the previous year. Charles summarizes the Doctrine in this way:

> The Doctrine of Discovery is the Church in Europe saying to the nations of Europe, whatever lands you find not ruled by Christian rulers, those people are less than human and their lands are yours for the taking. Charles goes on to say, "It was the Doctrine of Discovery that justified European nations colonizing Africa and enslaving the African people".[25]

The Second Vatican Council document *Lumen gentium* 17 sought to redress the Church's record of trampling on local culture. It states that the Church "fosters and assumes the ability, resources and customs of each people . . . Whatever good lies latent in the religious practices and cultures of diverse peoples, it is not only saved from destruction but it is also cleansed, raised up and made perfect unto the glory of God . . . "

Nostra Aetate (the Declaration on the Relation of the Church with Non-Christian Religions of the Second Vatican Council, promulgated on 28 October 1965 by Pope Paul VI) calls on the Church to "recognize, preserve and promote the good things, spiritual and moral, as well as the socio-cultural values found among" non-Christian religions.

The Catholic International Theological Commission of 1988 states: "Culture, which is always a concrete and particular culture, is open to the higher values common to all. Thus the originality of a culture does not signify withdrawal into itself but a contribution to the richness which is the good of all."[26]

In 1992, Pope John Paul II commended inculturation in his encyclical letter *Redemptoris missio*. He connected inculturation with the incarnation of the Gospel: "Through inculturation the church makes the Gospel incarnate in different cultures."[27]

He told indigenous Australians at Alice Springs in 1986: "The Church in Australia will not be fully the Church that Jesus wants her to be until you have made your contribution to her life and until that contribution has been received by others."[28] Australians who live the Celtic tradition point out how different things would be if the first missionaries from Europe had been Celtic monks.

Members of The Community of Aidan and Hilda in various lands have grasped this key to our future. The Revd Jack Stapleton, its first USA guardian, wrote in June 1995: "The US Chapter appears to be called to reconciliation work among the native peoples of our land . . . This was based on the understanding that our mission for the healing of the land would inevitably address local issues."[29] In South Africa, Bishop Eric Pike wrote an article which noted profound resonance between aspects of Xhosa and Celtic spirituality. In Australia, Brad Bessell wrote:

> Under our South Australian desert is the great artesian basin filled with millions of litres of water. The same could be said about the soul of this nation. It seems that church here looks for its nourishment from the seasonal rains that blow in from other countries. It comes and it goes and the land (church) is dry again. I believe that the Celtic Spirituality is not a seasonal rain or trend but something that is deeply buried under the Australian soul like our artesian waters under the desert. It is in the blood of the Scottish, Irish, Welsh, English convicts and immigrants. It just needs to be tapped. I believe that the role of Celtic Spirituality in this nation is to bring healing and reconciliation between the Aboriginal and Non-Aboriginal. In fact, I believe that had Celtic monks come to Australia then the Aboriginal people would have had a spiritual experience similar to that of the ancient Celtic Christians. I also believe the role of the Celtic renewal in this nation is to encourage the Church to embrace a faith that is more gentle and incarnational than the colonial one that we have inherited from our English forebears and less 'salesman-like' than the recent American models that we seem to have embraced.

The failure of the Synod of Whitby must be a spur to us to honour and celebrate local culture.

CHAPTER 3

Reality, roots, rhythms, relationship—
Four Rs of Celtic Christianity

The word "Celtic" has the capacity to excite wide disagreements in the general public and in academics alike. The reason is that whereas the words "Roman", "Greek" or "European" mean the same thing, the word "Celtic" means different things.

At the close of a lecture I gave in Norway on "Celtic Christianity", two archaeologists took me to task for using the word "Celtic" to describe a current movement within Christianity. The word "Celtic", they informed me, is properly used by archaeologists to describe the culture identified through artefacts found in Hallstadt in Austria and La Tène in Switzerland. A European Iron Age culture was named after the archaeological site of La Tène on the north side of Lake Neuchâtel in Switzerland, where thousands of objects had been deposited in the lake, as was discovered after the water level dropped in 1857. This culture describes the culture and art of Celtic peoples in these areas. It is often distinguished from earlier and neighbouring cultures mainly by the La Tène style of Celtic art, characterized by curving, "swirly" decoration, especially of metalwork.

La Tène culture developed and flourished during the late Iron Age (from about 500 BC to the Roman conquest in the first century BC) in Belgium, eastern France, Switzerland, Austria, southern Germany, the Czech Republic, Poland, Slovakia, Slovenia, Croatia and parts of Hungary, Ukraine and Romania, and eventually in Spain and Britain. It precedes the coming of Christianity to Britain and Ireland. This cultural period is explored more fully in Duncan Barrow's *Rethinking Celtic Art*.[30]

Another school of thought claims that the term Celtic belongs to historians and should not be applied to spirituality. The term *Kelti* was used by Roman writers to describe the inhabitants of Gaul and Britain before and after the Roman conquest of Britain. Barry Cunliffe gives examples of this in his *The Ancient Celts*.[31] All are agreed that the inhabitants of Britain and Ireland did not use this term of themselves. They did not think of themselves as Celtic, though it remains unclear why classical writers such as Julius Caesar described them as "*Celti*" if they had not heard this term used by local people.

In 2015, Thames and Hudson published *Blood of the Celts: The New Ancestral Story* by James Manco.[32] This reveals that earlier attempts to trace historical and prehistorical movements using only modern DNA from living people have been proved to be dramatically wrong by findings from DNA in ancient skeletal remains. In the twentieth century, anglophone archaeologists argued that the word "Celtic" should not be used about inhabitants of Britain, but recent DNA advances make this questionable.

During this century, a burst of archaeological projects has established that there were Celtic peoples on a far wider scale than was previously imagined. Simon Young describes some of these developments in his book *The Celtic Revolution: In Search of 2000 Forgotten Years that Changed the World*. He writes:

> Archaeological and linguistic evidence suggest that a large part of Celtica, as this area is sometimes called, shared the same style of possessions and art. And a better understanding of the religious customs of this area hints that the inhabitants had broadly similar spiritual traditions; while the very few clues that exist concerning their social organization point to a sense of oneness among the tribes there. The Celts, in short, did exist.[33]

Their area included the Roman province of Galatia to which the apostle Paul addressed his letter, and much of modern-day Turkey and Europe. The Celts were not called "the fathers of Europe" for nothing. This Celtic swathe did not, however, long survive the Roman armies. They were driven west to Britain and Ireland.

A third school, which I think is now the majority view, is that the word "Celtic" describes a group of languages that were spoken by people mainly in Gaul, Britain and Ireland before and during the early Christian centuries. They had related alphabets. The Brythonic Celtic languages were (and are) used in Brittany (Breizh), Cornwall (Kernow) and Wales (Cymru). The Goidelic or Gaelic Celtic languages are spoken in Ireland, Scotland and the Isle of Man. Within the Anglican/Episcopal Communion of Churches, the term "The Celtic Bishops" is now used to describe the biennial conference of the bishops in the provinces of all Ireland, Scotland and Wales.

The term "Celtic" is used in politics to describe the six or seven so-called "Celtic nations": Brittany, Cornwall, Galicia, Ireland, Isle of Man, Scotland and Wales. These are so-called because a minority still use a Celtic language, and they retain some distinctive cultural traits. These like to assume that the English are outsiders, but in 2006 an Oxford University research team claimed that many of the English also have "Celtic DNA".

Language purists object to terms such as "Celtic Spirituality" being used to describe movements of art, culture or religion, because they do not fall into any of the above categories. This objection takes no account of other valid disciplines such as the study of social phenomena. Such movements take real or imagined elements from cultures during the period when Celtic tongues were the first language and allow them to "take off" in a contemporary context. Thus, Celtic art and Celtic poetry feature in various revivals, as do pagan and Christian practices. This use of language to describe schools of thought, traditions and movements of art, culture or religion is widespread across the world and in most cultures. Some of it is fake, or at least nostalgic, but not all.

A typical criticism is that people pick and choose which bits of the Celtic tradition they regard as normative or appealing and fit these into self-centred lives that avoid the challenge implicit in the total reality. J. R. R. Tolkien said that "the term Celtic is a magic bag into which anything new may be put, and out of which almost anything may come. Anything is possible in the fabulous Celtic twilight, which is not so much a twilight of the gods as of reason."[34]

In this understanding, Celtic Christianity can mean anything that people want it to mean. I think there is truth in this criticism. For example, a well-known contemporary network of churches made Celtic spirituality the theme of one of its gatherings. A friend of mine who attended asked what place ascetics and hermits played in "the package". "We don't do hermits," he was told.

It should, however, be borne in mind that most postmodern people deconstruct history because they think all historians have selected facts to fit their own worldview and agendas. Thus, the meta narratives of religions and societies have often been male and elitist. Top people have written the narrative from a top person's point of view.

In some periods, the Celtic movement became welded to nationalism. In the nineteenth century, it became a vehicle for a romantic and poetic movement in reaction to the drabness of the industrialization of society. Some followers of this Celtic Twilight movement were neo-pagan, others were free-thinking, but others were believers of a sort.

At times, the Celtic label has been attached to movements of culture or art. In modern times, this is sometimes a cheap branding ploy, but often there is some continuity with the authentic ongoing tradition. Celtic Symbols on Pinterest is a marketing operation that draws on neo-pagan and narcissistic elements more than Christian—interweaving, spirals, the triquetra, also known as the Trinity knot, which resembles the ouroboros, an ancient infinity symbol. The triquetra is constructed of one continuous line interweaving around itself, symbolizing no beginning or end, an eternal spiritual life. The Celts believed that everything important in the world came in threes; three stages of life, three elements, three domains; earth, sea and sky; past, present and future. The triquetra is sometimes drawn weaving around a circle, symbolizing the unity of the three parts.

An internet search for "Celtic crafts" or "Celtic art" in fact reveals considerable cohesion of design; for example, knotwork, spirals, the triquetra. In pagan mythology, this symbolizes the three faces of the goddess and celebrates the feminine. In traditional Christian mythology, it symbolizes the Trinity, which has been taught within a patriarchal framework.

It is true that the fickle world of publishing climbed on to the Celtic bandwagon and gave a Celtic label to material that did not require it. When my publisher Kevin Mayhew asked me to compile *The Celtic Hymnbook*, I assembled a group of Scottish and Irish musicians and theologians to explore what we meant by "Celtic hymns". In the introduction to *The Celtic Hymnbook* I explained that the current rise of "Celtic" worship songs is rightly not restricted to the so-called "six Celtic nations" of Brittany, Wales, Cornwall, Ireland, Isle of Man and Scotland. For one thing, the Celts originated in Asia and spread throughout Europe's heartlands; for another, Celtic missions such as that of Aidan to English-speaking people introduced a distinctive spirituality to races that were not Celtic. Features which are distinctive, though not exclusive, to this trans-ethnic Celtic spirituality include penitence, pilgrimage, poetry, praise and passion; God's homeliness and presence in creation; blessing and lament; the Trinity. Celts see hymns as a way of winging earth-bound mortals into heaven. So, even when neither the words nor the music come from one of these six "nations", earthed hymns that notably combine several of these features are included. Conversely, famous hymn writers from these six lands are excluded if they are prisoner to one of the separated strands which are neither holistic nor rooted, as are many of the current glut of worship songs that cash in on the label "Celtic" but which divorce Jesus from the Trinity, justice from faith and people from the web of life:

> What is Celtic music? The lilt of Irish tunes, the syncopation of Scottish ballads, the fire and flow of Welsh community songs may all be recognized in this selection. Celtic music tends to be modal: in ancient times there were various modes, or scales, each with five notes. There is a preference for the pentatonic scale. The Lament and the Anthem are distinctive features: Anthems are a strong call to battle. Typical Celtic instruments include pipes, fiddles, bodhran, whistle, strings and harp. Such instruments were common among ancient peoples who were in touch with primal drives. Both the bagpipe and the harp are mentioned in the Book of Daniel (3:7). Such instruments link us with the elements: human breath is linked to the breath of God; the vibrating harp strings pluck both the air and the heart. Such instruments are an enrichment, though the hymns in this book may be sung without them.

> The Celtic vision is that we join as one in "the song of all creation". The world calls us to develop an intimate relationship between the body (lips, throat, lungs) and the spirit (breath). Singing helps to bring this about. Hildegard of Bingen observed that singing words reveals their true meaning directly to the soul through bodily vibrations.[35]

The Iona Community is sometimes perceived by outsiders to be in the Celtic tradition. This is partly because it hosts programmes on the iconic island of Iona, forever associated with St Columba, and partly because the Wild Goose Resources Group, with which it is closely associated, publishes many Scottish genre songs by John Bell and others. However, some of its members robustly disassociate themselves from the label "Celtic", because they wish to disentangle evangelical and charismatic elements from their commitment to justice, and to de-mythologize the miraculous from accounts of early Celtic leaders. A few years ago, the Community seriously considered withdrawing from Iona in order to focus on justice and its priority work in needy parts of Glasgow.

The criticism that proponents of Celtic spirituality are selective with the facts can be levelled at most parts of the Christian Church and at most movements of thought throughout history. In an age when social media create addictions to prejudice, we need to guard against a dismissive attitude to anything outside our comfort zone.

In 2000, Handsel Press published Donald Meek's *The Quest for Celtic Christianity*. This offers a sustained review and critique of present-day expressions of "Celtic Christianity". Donald Meek is a Gaelic-speaking native of the Hebridean island of Tiree and a Baptist steeped in the Reformed tradition. He was educated at the universities of Glasgow (MA and PhD in Celtic Studies) and Cambridge (MA in Anglo-Saxon, Norse and Celtic) and at the time of writing was Professor of Celtic at Aberdeen University. His world is that of ancient languages, and his worldview is informed by the Reformation tradition within Gaelic-speaking islands. So the eruption of a spiritual dynamic from places far removed from his landscape, which people yet label "Celtic", which includes charismatic and ecumenical elements and, worse still, English Christians who speak no Celtic language, must seem strange indeed, and perhaps explains the tone of irritation which pervades his book.

His stated purpose is twofold: to expose the warps and weaknesses of modern interpretations of Celtic Christianity, and to point to more reliable ways of perceiving and assessing the real achievements and qualities of the Christian faith in the British Isles in the early Middle Ages. He claims that belief in ecumenism, feminism and tolerance is frequently paraded in contemporary Celtic spirituality when, in fact, all three are "figments of contemporary counter-cultural imagination".[36]

He judges that the drivers of popular "Celtic Christianity" are mainly from English-based metropolitan culture, devoid of a Celtic language or culture themselves, that they react negatively to much in contemporary society and Church and attribute certain contrastingly positive positions to "Celtic Christianity". He accuses such people of misappropriating Celtic symbols and the term "Celtic".

Within his own terms Meek's points bear scrutiny. But are his the only appropriate terms to use in an attempt to define "Celtic"? The "concoction" (is this a less than objective term for "anthology"?) in fact includes prayers from his own Hebridean islands, but that is incidental. A key question that he fails to ask is: must spiritual and social phenomena be defined only by the ethnic and language categories with which their origins are linked?

Two fellow academics, one Scottish and one Welsh, address this issue in a major volume published about the same time. The publisher of *The Classics of Western Spirituality*, which it describes as "in one series, the original writings of the universally acknowledged teachers of the Catholic, Protestant, Eastern Orthodox, Jewish and Islamic traditions", saw fit to include a volume entitled *Celtic Spirituality*.[37] In his preface to this book, James P. Mackey of the Faculty of Divinity at Edinburgh University, refers to the contention that there is no such thing as Celtic Christianity. He argues that the case for it is based on what might be called the principle of inculturation and on the evidence of a culture shared by a loose family of peoples. The inculturation principle states that Christianity, like any other religion, inevitably takes the shape of the culture—the images, ideas, practices and institutions—in which it is born or to which it travels. It is shaped in the mutations formed in the concrete and local, but then "the ones that promise life more abundant spread into other concrete locales in a mutual or rather multiple-interactive process".

Oliver Davies (then Reader in Philosophical Theology at the University of Wales) reminds us in his introduction that anthropologists have coined the terms *emic* and *etic* identities. Emic refers to the identity a particular group holds with respect to itself, etic to that which others place on it. Most of the cultural and ethnic categories that historians habitually employ function at the etic level and not at the emic one. Thus, we speak of "American history" before people would have dreamed of calling themselves "American", and "British history" extends back to a period many centuries before the emergence of the modern British state.

In other contexts, would claims that people outside one's own ethnic or language group could play no part in something that has grown out of that group be regarded as a form of racism?

Perhaps a much-diluted form of this ethnic prejudice comes from certain Anglo-Catholic scholars. Benedicta Ward's *High King of Heaven*[38] and Paul Cavill's *Anglo-Saxon Christianity*,[39] both published in 1999, object that characteristics defined as "Celtic" in popular books, such as monastic prayer, close awareness of saints and heaven, and high crosses, belong as much to Anglo-Saxon, or English Christianity, as to Celtic.

This objection seems to assume that the Irish influence was not a strand in Anglo-Saxon religion, and a major contributor to the conversion of the pagan English to Christianity. A large amount of these writers' material comes from the largest Anglo-Saxon kingdom of Northumbria, which owed its conversion to the Irish Mission led by St Aidan from Iona. The Bewick and Ruthwell crosses, the large number of monasteries, the honouring of saints such as Cuthbert, and the Lindisfarne Gospels are largely, though not entirely, the flower of the Irish Mission. In a way, they pay tribute to the Irish Mission, which worked cross-culturally so effectively that, after its withdrawal, the seeds that it had planted rooted and sprouted among the English.

In his *Ecclesiastical History of the English People*, Bede writes of Angles and Saxons as the settlers and rulers of the area that later became known as England, and of Romans and Irish as missionaries, some of whom settled.[40] He also mentions Irish who married into ruling Saxon families. He disdains the ("Celtic") Britons whose kingdoms remained to the west of the English and skimps over the Britons who remained as peasants in areas ruled by Anglo-Saxons.

I am not aware of popular Celtic writers who have described an Anglo-Saxon kingdom as a Celtic kingdom, although David Adam does posit, mainly on the basis of reflective intuition, that some of the Christian foundations in Northumbria such as Melrose, which most scholars assume were founded by Aidan's mission, were in fact pre-existing British Celtic foundations.[41] It is true, however, that in books about Celtic spirituality many write about saints such as Aidan, Oswald, Cuthbert and Hilda in Anglo-Saxon kingdoms. Is this valid?

It is generally recognized by scholars that the pagan Anglo-Saxon colonizers were evangelized in the seventh century by two major missions: that from Rome, spearheaded from Canterbury in the south (Augustine arrived in Kent in 593), and that from the Irish, via Iona, spearheaded from Lindisfarne in the north (Aidan arrived in 635). Aidan evangelized Northumbria, the largest of the English kingdoms. His patron, the devout King Oswald, who was brought up by the Irish in Dalriada and had a child by an Irish mother, whose Irish warriors helped to secure his throne, became the leading king among the English, and through missions, alliances, intermarriages and conquests spread his faith tradition into the English heartlands and to the south. Following the Synod of Whitby in 664, the Roman regulatory framework was adopted by the English kingdoms and Lindisfarne's Irish monks departed to Ireland. Yet Irish bishops and missionaries continued after that, and people whose spirituality owed much to the Irish continued to shape English life. Cuthbert and Hilda stand out among these, but these two giants espoused many apprentices.

Aldfrith, whose mother was Irish and who was a monk at Iona, ruled the Saxon kingdom of Northumbria for almost twenty years from 685 to 705. Until his accession he had been a Christian scholar trained in the Irish tradition; after it, he became a patron of the arts and during his reign work on the Lindisfarne Gospels was begun. He helped to ensure that the Irish tradition brought by Aidan continued to be influential long after his death.

Some fine scholars of the early Church in Anglo-Saxon England, such as Benedicta Ward, have complained that people have been misled into thinking that this is part of "the Celtic Church". In her book *High King of*

Heaven: Aspects of Early English Spirituality, she sympathetically traces how the "Mediterranean" and the "Irish" strands combine to create a distinctive English spirituality. She explains that the title of her book is about the "English" rather than the "Anglo-Saxon", since the latter term may suggest a contrast with "Celtic", and "it seems that these terms are best understood by relationship rather than by contrast. There is at present an idea that early English Christianity involved triumphalist Roman missionaries in conflict with the simple Celts, British and Irish."[42] She then quotes the following from Edmund Bishop's *Liturgica Historica*:

> In the devotional products of the first period the Irishman and the Roman are pouring their respective pieties into the devoted isle and we absorb both kinds: but the English mind and religious sense assert themselves in the process of fusion and contribute to the resultant a quality and measure possessed neither by Celt nor Roman alone. I seem to discern as the specifically "English" quality of this earliest devotional literature, strong feeling controlled and also permeated by good sense.[43]

Many Roman Catholics fail to see a problem in this matter. The late Cardinal Basil Hume loved monk bishops such as Aidan and Cuthbert, but their distinctiveness was in their person more than in their patronage, which is why he also included Bede and Benedict Biscop from the Roman tradition. He taught that Celtic spirituality was one of the three strands in English Catholicism.

> Listen to me, you that pursue righteousness, you that seek the LORD. Look to the rock from which you were hewn, and to the quarry from which you were dug.
>
> *Isaiah 51:1*

We have agreed that the word "Celtic" can be used for ephemeral fancies. But this begs the question as to whether there is a core beneath the fancies. The prophets Isaiah and Jeremiah called upon their peoples to mine from the quarry from which they were formed by God. "Celtic" is not a single definition word; it embraces a spectrum. But in this spectrum, as in a rainbow, there are principles of coherence. If, as Ian Bradley concludes in his *Following the Celtic Way*, the word "Celtic" may properly be used to describe the Christianity of peoples in Britain and Ireland who spoke a Celtic language in the fourth to seventh centuries (for purists) or up to the twelfth century (for others), it is possible to identify some distinctive (though not unique) characteristics.[44] Some of these characteristics resurface in various fresh expressions of this Celtic Christianity through succeeding centuries.

It is the settled conviction of many thoughtful people that the Celtic tradition holds elements that the Western Church lost, some of which the Eastern Church retained—and that the recovery of this tradition is a key to redeeming Western Christianity, healing the schism between East and West, and restoring the Jesus movement on earth as a Way.

One characteristic that refuses to be extinguished is the "unsanitized" nature of Celtic spirituality. I sent a draft Night Prayer for a retreat in a church in south-east England. This begins, reflecting words in *The Carmina Gadelica*: "I lie down this night with Christ and Christ will lie down with me." The retreat organizer reworded it as "I lie down near Christ . . . " We don't want a Christ who gets into bed with us!

On 21 June 1994, Simon Barrington Ward, then Bishop of Coventry, welcomed the leaders of the nascent Community of Aidan and Hilda, who draw inspiration from early Celtic saints, to his home. He said:

> Western people are split. We need a model of wholeness. We can't
> go back as if individualization had never happened . . . we must
> go forward through a repentance and a spirituality of the Cross
> and resurrection that involves deep listening to the people in
> our neighbourhoods. I am excited by everything you are doing.[45]

Donald Meek dismisses the 1990s' fresh expressions of Celtic Christianity as originating in an English metropolitan culture. Yet one of the earliest of these "Celtic" writers, David Adam, was a former coal miner and a Northumbrian born and bred. The rock band Iona, which included an Irish singer, launched their first track in 1990.

Many of those who responded to the decade's new ideas were evangelicals or charismatics who sensed there was something more, but pagans who sought Jesus were also drawn, and Catholics as well as Protestants. Cardinal Basil Hume's TV series and book spoke to many.[46]

Before any of these, in 1972 Professor John Macquarrie drew attention in *Paths in Spirituality* to the Gaelic awareness of God's immanence in the world, his involvement with nature and with the world, and his nearness to us. He contrasted this with the more dominant stress in the Western world on God's transcendence. He stated:

> I doubt very much whether the quest (for a vision of the world in a new wholeness and depth) can be fulfilled unless we can realise again . . . the sense of presence . . . The Celt was very much a God-intoxicated man whose life was embraced on all sides by the Divine Being.[47]

In May 2003, Grove Books published my small book *Celtic Spirituality: Rhythm, Roots and Relationships*.[48] This, too, became a bestseller and was re-printed. In this book I set out three universal principles—Rhythm, Roots and Relationships—and drew from the early Church in Celtic-speaking lands distinctive ways in which these principles were applied that can enrich people today. I argued that praying daily in the rhythm of the sun is part of the birth right of Jews, Christians and Muslims, but today's Western Christians have neglected this practice because of the avalanche of counter attractions, and perhaps because of the over-clericalization of the Church. The early Church in Celtic lands had a larger monastic and tribal component than did churches elsewhere in Europe, and new monasticism is seeking to re-establish this practice.

I highlighted roots because the way of life that comes to us through the writings of Patrick, the histories of Bede, and the hagiographies of saints suggests that believers were soaked in Scriptures, in the holy lives of martyrs and saintly teachers, and in prayer. There was nothing unique about this, but it forms a rich vein in God's treasury. What I wrote about relationships focused on the nature of churches as local communities and on the role of the soul friend.

One key to genuine spirituality is the willingness to uncover truth wherever it may be found and to respond to it wherever it may lead. A genuine seeker after the spirituality of the early Celtic Christians has to take seriously the ascetic practices as well as the loveable traits and to see through our commodified society to the holistic basis of Celtic Christianity.

A Celtic spirituality without disciplines and regular practices is indeed a leaf blown by the wind. However, there is abundant evidence of spiritual disciplines which provide some continuity with the past and which give substance to the present. So to be valid, use of the terms Celtic Christianity or Celtic spirituality must show either that some guiding Christian principles from the early churches in Celtic-speaking lands can be identified and applied today, or that there has been some, albeit fragmentary, continuity between ancient and contemporary Celtic-speaking areas from which a distinctive expression of art or spirituality flows.

The Acts of the Apostles describes how Christianity began in a Jewish container and spread to a dualistic Greek culture. In the following centuries, the Church grew in imperial power. Manual workers were lower than the clergy and ceased to be treated as brothers and sisters in one family. Clergy were "head" people. The heart became marginalized. There was a separation between head, heart and hands. When Christianity spread to the Celtic fringes of Europe, this might be called The Acts of the Apostles Volume 2—a third way, which is as much part of the universal Christian tradition as the first two (the Jewish and Greek cultures). Manual workers, teachers and students, and mystics who made vigils were part of the furniture of the one monastic family. The unity of head, heart and hands is not fake, it is a foundational principle. The Bible, the Spirit and Justice remain three fundamental elements of Celtic Christianity.

I use the word "Celtic" to embrace several inalienable aspects of the first Celtic Mission. It is indigenous, cross-cultural, guttural, incarnational. Brent Lyons Lee urged that we include in our book *Celtic Spirituality in an Australian Landscape* this "snapshot" of Celtic spirituality:

> Hospitality. No gender bias. An anti-empire mindset. Loving nature and God's creation. Being open to learning from the saints. A focus on the Trinity: the divine community. Creating space for art. Poetry and story-telling. Communing with God in wild

or elemental places; Fostering monasteries (churches) that are villages of God.[49]

In his book *The Death of Truth*, Michito Kakutani traces our present post-truth culture, where anything can be labelled fake news, to the rise of postmodernism, with its insistence that "everything is just a construct", as well as to the "new narcissism" and the social media revolution of misinformation and relativism.[50]

We in the Celtic new monastic tradition, along with many others, call people to follow the Way, the Truth and the Life. This assumes that, although religions and philosophies are coloured by the lens through which we view them—our own and our culture's sometimes unconscious narcissism or ignorance—it is possible to strip them to their inalienable core which passes the tests of scrutiny, time, transition and authenticity.

A retreatant said to me, "Celtic is just a manifestation in a particular time of what God wants to bring about all the time." The apostle Paul wrote: "Consider your own call, brothers and sisters: not many of you were wise by human standards, not many were powerful, not many were of noble birth" (1 Corinthians 1:26). This expression of Celtic Christianity was a return to the humility of the grassroots.

Christianity is a call to strip off all that is fake, and to become aware of what is eternally real, to exercise the core. It calls us to roots, rhythms, relationships and reality. It helps us become fit for purpose.

CHAPTER 4

Weave together Christianity's separated strands—catholic, biblical, charismatic, communal

Two different kinds of critic say there is no such thing as the Celtic Church. 1) The first kind claims that there was no Celtic Church because the church of each tribe or monastic family was different, so there were no characteristics that were common to Britain or Ireland as a whole. 2) The second kind claims that there was one, worldwide catholic or Roman church, and that there were no common distinguishing marks of the church in a Celtic country.

1) Scholars such as Wendy Davies, in her essay "The Myth of the Celtic Church", try to ferret out early church practices and organization in Ireland that differed from those in Britain, or between different kingdoms or monastic families within each country, to justify her assertion that there was no such thing as "the Celtic Church", because the church of each tribe or region was different. For example, she suggests some faith communities in Wales used pre-Gregorian liturgy which seems absent in Ireland. She weakens her case by pointing out that there were also divergences of custom in "the continental church" and by using the phrase "insular church" to distinguish the church in Celtic lands from the church on the continental mainland.[51]

The argument which Markus and others have made, that church members in different kingdoms in Celtic lands had little or no intercourse with church members in other kingdoms, is surely false. It is thought there may have been an archbishop for the four late Roman provinces in Britain, at London, York, Lincoln and Cirencester. The three bishops who attended the 314 Council of Arles from three of these cities must have communicated with each other. It is known that Patrick brought British evangelists with him to Ireland. David of Wales welcomed Irish monks to stay at his monasteries, such as the young Aidan and Modomnoc, who was commissioned to take the monastery's beehive back to bless Ireland. Many Irish monastic founders studied for a time at Whithorn, as did those in Wales. Others besides Ninian stayed at Tours and brought the teaching of Martin of Tours back to Britain and Ireland. Sea routes from Ireland to Wales and Cornwall and vice versa were routinely used by traders, missionaries and monks. Cornwall has innumerable foundations of saints who travelled there from other parts of Celtic lands. Pilgrimage was beloved of Christians in different Celtic tribes, and monasteries were famed for their hospitality to pilgrims.

2) The opposite argument, which Gilbert Markus makes in "The End of Celtic Christianity", is that Gaels never thought of themselves as separate from the authority of the Bishop of Rome and that their bishops were hierarchical.[52]

Markus points out that the *Collectio Canonum Hibernensis* 20:3 has Patrick declaring that if "any questions arise in this island, let them be referred to the apostolic see". But this was an eighth-century collection that appeared in Gaul at a time when Rome was extending and codifying its powers, and is thought to reflect a view of the pro-Roman party within the Irish church. The only other quote he can find is from the time when the see of Armagh was setting out its claim to jurisdiction over Ireland, and decreed that if it could not settle a case it be sent to the see of Rome.[53] This dates to 734, and does not represent earlier views or views from other parts of Ireland or Britain. It overlooks the fact that the Council of Ephesus in 431 decreed that churches beyond the Roman Empire (which at that date included both Britain and Ireland) were free to follow their own patterns. Bede himself records Augustine of Canterbury saying to the British bishops:

> If you will comply with me in these three matters, to wit, to keep Easter at the due time; to fulfil the ministry of Baptism, by which we are born again to God, according to the custom of the holy Roman Apostolic Church; and to join with us in preaching the

> Word of God to the English nation, we will gladly suffer all the
> other things you do, though contrary to our customs.[54]

This argument also overlooks British Bishop Diaothus's reply to Augustine
on the authority of Rome in Britain:

> We are . . . prepared to defer to the Church of God, and to the
> Bishop of Rome . . . so far as to love everyone in perfect charity,
> and to assist them all by word and deed in becoming children of
> God. This deference we are willing to pay to him, as to every other
> Christian, but as for any other obedience, we know of none that
> he, whom you term the Pope or Bishop of Bishops, can demand.[55]

From the fragmentary evidence we have (see, for example, the First
Synod of the Bishops, namely Patrick, Auxilius, Isernius)[56] it is true that
St Patrick tried to establish an ecclesiastical system that included rules
laid down by the Bishop of Rome.

People who collected for charity without higher permission were
banned from the church; if a charity collector had a surplus, he was to lay
it on the bishop's altar. Any cleric whose hair was not shorn in the Roman
manner, or whose wife went about with head unveiled, were removed
from the Church. If a priest had built a church, he should not offer the
holy sacrifice in it until a bishop had come to consecrate it, and so on.

This gives the lie to contemporary independent "Celtic" churches
which refuse to be accountable in any way to the wider Body of Christ.

Those two realities (the honour due to the Bishop of Rome and the
hierarchical nature of bishops), however, leave much space for distinctive
developments to flourish. For long periods Britain and Ireland were cut
off from Rome. It seems leaders such as Columbanus assumed that going
all out for God was the best way of supporting the bishops. They assumed
that if they were going all out, they were pleasing the bishop who was
commissioned to go all out for God.

It is true that Christianity was introduced to parts of Britain in the first
three Christian centuries by soldiers of Rome's occupying army, as well
as by traders to seaports outside the occupied areas. It seems, according
to legends and inscriptions, that some of these ships brought missionary

pilgrims from Egypt who were not under the jurisdiction of the Pope. Other churches were planted in the spirit of the counter-church culture of Gaul's Martin of Tours—followers of Martin established cells. In Britain and Ireland these were often known as White Houses, after the name given to Martin's cells at Ligugé.

Several factors lead us to the conclusion that the early church in Ireland was not locked into monochrome legalism. Patrick, in his *Confession*, affirms that he appointed 153 bishops who were all filled with the Holy Spirit. The First Synod's list of decisions made clear that banishments could be ended following penance by the wrongdoer. These bishops were so open to the Spirit and to the patterns of the indigenous people that within a few generations that church was organized along tribal and monastic lines, and bishops were part of a monastic community under the authority of their spiritual father, the abbot.

Prophetic and healing gifts flourished, initiatives were taken, fresh faith communities were founded under direct inspiration from the Holy Spirit.

Bede clearly distinguishes (not always favourably) between the indigenous church that existed in Britain before Pope Gregory sent his Roman Mission to Kent in 597 and the latter. He writes also about distinctive marks of the Irish church. He is critical of some of its provincial customs on the one hand, but admiring of the sanctity of its Christians on the other hand.

In 371, a crowd came to Ligugé and forcibly carried Martin to the neighbouring diocese of Tours which was electing a new bishop. Those who looked for a dignitary, including the visiting bishops who would consecrate the elected candidate, despised this shabby nonentity, but the people elected him. At his consecration he exchanged a throne for a cow stool, and soon afterwards left his palatial quarters to live in a cave on the north bank of the River Loire, three miles upstream at Marmoutier. The cliffs were honeycombed with caves, like sand martins' nests. By 393, all these caves were inhabited by hermits, and the grassy plain below was covered by shacks inhabited by 2,000 mainly young men from noble families. In Tours was a smaller group of women. It was an experiment in Christian living in which those who were rich shared with those who were poor, maintaining a life of silence, punctuated by the times of prayer and service. Every autumn Martin toured the furthest outposts of his diocese in missionary journeys, accompanied by signs and wonders, and taught his disciples to teach both agriculture and the Faith to the uneducated people.

Thirteen years after Martin's death in 397, the last Roman troops left Britain. The Church was a weak rump amid a pantheon of gods and half-beliefs. The British landowners, who had married and worked with the Romans, assumed a chequered leadership that was threatened by invasions from pagan Picts, Irish and Saxons. One of these Romano-Britons, Ninian, journeyed to Rome to be trained and ordained a bishop. On the way home he stayed at Tours and was never the same again. He resolved that he, too, would establish a colony of heaven—this time on British soil. He imported from Martin of Tours' community not just masons, but Christian brothers and also the names of Martin's houses. Candida Casa is simply a translation of Leuko-Teiac (Bright White Hut), the name of the bothy on Bishop Hilary's farm near Ligugé, where Martin first organized his family of Christians, whence today's Whithorn gets its name. Whithorn grew into a village of God: celibates, families, those in vows and others were all part of the community. Some of them met maybe five times each day and three times each night to pray. This community acted as a hotel, a hospital, a school and a creative arts centre. All the trades needed for a self-sustaining community were there: metal-, glass- and wood-craft, baking and brewing. They cleared trees and stones and drained land in order to grow crops, rear livestock and farm fish. They encouraged personal spiritual development with a soul friend and engaged in pastoral care and conflict resolution in their region. They allowed themselves to be disciplined.

According to Daphne Brooke, archaeological evidence suggests that Ninian's Candida Casa (Shining White House) was not merely inspired by the example of Martin, but could have been a daughter colony of Marmoutier or Ligugé.[57]

Archibald Scott argues that Ninian's house was unlikely to have been as grand as later writers made out. It was more likely to have been a modest house suited for prayer and sacraments at small gatherings. This view is supported by the references to this White House when Paulinus of York and Alcuin provided help to preserve it. Such White Houses are found associated with Celtic churches from Dornoch in the north of Pictland to Ty Gwyn ar Dav among Britons in Wales. It is believed that Ninian established places like these White Houses in the shires of Ayr, Glasgow, Forfar, Aberdeen, Inverness, Sutherland and right up to the Orkney Islands. Ninian divided much of Pictland into districts, at the hub of which was often one of these White Houses. These formed one family, or dispersed community, who looked to the White House in Galloway as their mother house.

According to tradition, the most important Romano-British family further south was located in what is now Wales, and belonged to Maximus, the Roman general who married the British princess Helena. He deposed the Arian Emperor, was declared emperor by his British troops, and established his family at Treves. There the family met Martin of Tours, whose monks were busy transforming the land and peasants of rural Gaul. So great was Martin's influence on their son, Publicius (the Welsh call him Peblig), that after his father was killed by the Emperor of the East, the family settled in Wales and established, at Llanbeblig, what was probably the first of over 500 monastic settlements.

James Kenney makes the important point that, although Celtic Christianity was not in any way a breakaway branch of the Church, there were some key cultural differences that caused friction:

> Fundamentally, the Church in Ireland was one with the Church in the remainder of Western Europe. The mental processes and the *Weltanschauung* of the ecclesiastic who looked out from Armagh or Clonmacnois or Innisfallen were not essentially different from those of him whose center of vision was Canterbury or Reims or Cologne. But in many important aspects, and particularly those of organization and of relationships with the secular powers, the Church in Ireland presented a marked variation from that on the Continent. These divergences were the occasion, in their own times, of friction culminating in accusations of heresy.[58]

Local churches in Britain and Ireland developed some common characteristics: monasticism, centred in a monastery under an abbot, who in some cases was allowed to marry and to transfer the monastery to his son; a strong missionary incentive; an emphasis on scholarship; a different tonsure from that of Roman monks; and a different way of setting the date of Easter, to name a few.

Although I think it is valid to speak of "the church in Celtic-speaking lands" in the first millennium, and to use the phrase "the Celtic Church" as a short-hand, I agree with critics who dismiss claims made by a myriad of self-proclaimed Celtic churches in the USA that they are resurrecting the "original, independent Celtic church", and with critics who dismiss Protestant claims that the original church in Celtic lands was Protestant. I have heard Northern Ireland Protestants claim this. German historian Lutz von Padberg coined the term "Iroschottisch" to describe this supposed dichotomy between Irish-Scottish and Roman Christianity.[59]

The USA, with its independent culture, has spawned a glut of independent churches and groups which call themselves "Celtic". Most of these hold a belief that there was once an independent "Celtic Church" that fought a gallant but losing battle against Romanization, and that equality between men and women is part of this heritage. There is a profusion of websites such as Celtic Christian Links and The Celtic Christian Communion.

Untenable and incompatible claims have indeed been made. Protestants have claimed that the early church in their land was Protestant in all but name. It was asserted that this church was independent of Rome, its only authority was the Bible, its leadership was home-grown, and its organization was locally determined. These claimants have confused autonomy with independence. Facts upon which the claim of independence was based are few.

Others, implausibly, trace Presbyterianism back to Columba, since he remained a presbyter rather than become a bishop. More plausibly, serious attempts have been made to trace Anglicanism back to the early Celtic period. Matthew Parker, Archbishop of Canterbury, published his *De Antiquitate Britannicae Ecclesiae* in 1572, and in 1631 James Usher, Archbishop of Armagh, published his *A Discourse of the Religion Anciently Professed by the Irish and the British*. What such works establish is that the Bishop of Rome had not yet accumulated powers to control what went on outside his own diocese. This is confirmed by the Council of Ephesus in 431, which declared that no bishop had the right to interfere with churches outside their jurisdiction. Churches outside the Empire were free to follow their own patterns. It does not, however, indicate that the churches in Britain and Ireland had no relationship with the universal Church. The attendance of three British bishops at the Council of Arles in 314 is evidence of that. The insular churches accepted the creeds and the biblical canon agreed by the universal Church. Independent Protestant claims to be heirs to early Celtic churches cannot be justified, because those in the Celtic churches regarded themselves as Catholic; they had priests ordained by bishops who were consecrated in the apostolic succession.

Pope Gregory the Great (590–604) famously wrote to Abbot Mellitus, who was on his way to join Augustine, Bishop of Canterbury:

> Tell Augustine that he should by no means destroy the temples of the gods but rather the idols within those temples. Let him, after he has purified them with holy water, place altars and relics of the saints in them. For, if those temples are well built, they should be converted from the worship of demons to the service of the true God. Thus, seeing that their places of worship are not destroyed, the people will banish error from their hearts and come to places familiar and dear to them in acknowledgement and worship of the true God.[60]

This was a letter from a brother which imposed nothing.

Pope Boniface V (619–25) wrote letters to Edwin, then the pagan King of Northumbria, whose wife was Christian. He sent gifts and pleaded with him to renounce idols and be baptized, but he claimed no jurisdiction. However, after Edwin's conversion Boniface's successor, Pope Honorius, in 634 sent a papal pallium to Paulinus as "Metropolitan of York" and another to his namesake Honorius of Canterbury. He thus exerted a moral but not a juridical influence.

Markus fails to mention the letter Columbanus wrote to Pope Boniface IV from Milan in 612:

> We are the disciples of St. Peter and St. Paul, and of the other holy men of God who, inspired by the Holy Ghost, wrote the sacred canon of the Scriptures. Dwelling in the ultimate places of the

earth, the Hibernians receive no other doctrine but that of the Gospel and of the Apostles. In our island there are no heretics, no Jews, no schismatics. Here the Catholic faith is preserved as intact as it was delivered to us by you, the successors of the Apostles ... Whatever I shall say that is orthodox and useful will redound to your honor: for is not the pure doctrine of the disciples the glory of the master? And when the son speaks wisely, does not the father rejoice? The river owes the purity of its water, not to itself, but to the source from which it springs ...

Watch over the peace of the Church; come to the aid of your sheep, terrified by the wolves; speak to them with the voice of the true Pastor; stand between them and the wolves, so that, laying aside all fear, they may recognize you as their true shepherd ... Be vigilant at your post day and night. If you do not wish to lose the honor due to your apostolic office, preserve the apostolic faith; confirm it by your testimony; fortify it by a written instrument; cover it with the authority of a synod, and no one will have the right to resist you. Do not, I entreat you, scorn this advice because it comes from a foreigner ... Those who have always remained true to the orthodox faith, even though they be your inferiors, will be your judges ...

Forgive me, if my harsh words have offended your pious ears. The freedom of discussion which is a characteristic of my native land is in part to blame for my boldness. Amongst us, not persons, but reasons, are weighed ... For only so long as right reason is on your side, will your authority remain undisputed: the true keeper of the keys of the Kingdom of Heaven is he who opens the gates to the worthy and closes them against the unworthy. If he did the contrary of this, he could neither open nor close. All the world knows that the Savior gave the keys of Heaven to St. Peter; but if you are puffed up on this account, and claim above others some unheard of power in divine things, remember that such presumption will lessen your authority in the sight of God.[61]

Reason, purity, truth, authenticity, not hierarchy, seem to be the values that create catholicity for Columbanus.

Only after the Fifth Ecumenical Council of Constantinople in 553 was it decreed that Rome's Pope had jurisdiction over Britain, but barbarian invasions cut off access to Rome for a longer period. Bede goes into the controversy over the date of Easter in detail. It seems that Pope Honorius, flexing his muscles prematurely, threatened excommunication if the Irish churches did not adopt the revised date of Easter. In a synod near Durrow in 630, southern Irish churches agreed to change the date, but other churches, notably the Columba family of churches, declined and were not in fact excommunicated, for as yet no pope had that power. What this tells us is that the churches of Celtic-speaking lands understood themselves to be part of the universal Church, which allowed them freedom to make their own decisions about customs and patterns of prayer.

In 680, the Pope appointed Theodore as Archbishop of Canterbury, who tried to create a common framework in the English church.

Protestants accuse Catholics of Romanizing the Church. Claims are often made that, in contrast, the Celtic tradition promotes indigenous patterns of church. Chris Seaton and Roger Ellis argue in *The New Celts* that the Celts' Christian apostles took local culture seriously.[62] The Second Vatican Council acknowledged the validity of allowing local cultures to flourish.[63]

What evidence is there for this belief that the Celtic approach encourages indigenous patterns? It is true that the different monastic families in the seventh-century British and Irish churches each had their own distinctive Rule and liturgy, but their liturgies drew from Gallic, Mozarabic and Roman, as well as local, rites. Certainly, their leaders were home-grown, in the sense that they were appointed from within the tribal leadership, though this hereditary principle had its own problems. An unsuitable descendant of a monastic founder might be appointed abbot instead of a more suitable, prayerful person. The eighth-century Celi De reform movement had to address this weakness.[64] Patrick gathered the leaders and preached Jesus's Gospel to them. Over the following months, as they witnessed signs and miracles, they bowed in obedience to God and Patrick. He gathered the senior chief Laeghaire, the chief bard, and the lawmakers of his part of Ireland. They set out the laws of Ireland, known as the Senchus Mor. It seems that some were written down at that time, but that most were handed down by word of mouth until the seventh century, when Cenn Faelad wrote them down. A wise man named Dubtach set out all the legal judgements that prevailed through the law of nature, and the law of the seers, and in the judgements delivered, and through the poets. They had foretold that the bright word of blessing would come, for it was the Holy Spirit who spoke through the mouths of these pagan lovers of justice, for the law of nature had prevailed where the written law did not reach.

Now they put together the true judgements that the Holy Spirit had spoken through the lawmakers and poets down to the reception of the faith of Jesus. What did not clash with the Word of God in the Old and New Testaments, and with the consciences of believers, was confirmed in the law of the Brehons by Patrick and the church leaders and chiefs of Ireland. For the law of nature had been right, except for the additions of the faith and the Church and its people.

The Irish understood that God was calling them to become a country organized according to laws revealed by God, but these enhanced, rather than obliterated, their existing laws.

I have sought to establish that the early churches in Celtic lands were part of the one, holy, catholic and apostolic church, as yet undivided, but that they were not monochrome. They went with local patterns and Spirit-led initiatives at a time before the Bishop of Rome took unilateral powers to standardize these things.

In 1995, Michael Mitton's book *Restoring the Woven Cord: Strands of Celtic Christianity for the Church today* was published.[65] In fourteen chapters he highlights these distinctive, though not unique, strands that were present in the one church, each exemplified in the life of a Celtic saint. These strands include authenticity, Bible, creativity, community, healing, holy dying, prayer, prophecy and spiritual combat. His choices reflect his role as a leader in charismatic renewal. In my writings I have added further strands, such as a sacramental view of creation, soul friendship and justice. Such strands are not unique, but they are distinctive. They appeal to people who seek a renewal of holistic faith and who are drawn by these God-intoxicated Celts.

An Amazon anonymous reader's review of Michael Mitton's book states:

In seeking—rightly—to restore validity to ancient Celtic Christianity, I think that Mitton ends up making the same mistakes as he criticises, i.e. failing to see the positive aspects of that which he criticises ('Roman' Christianity) and the negative aspects of that which he espouses.

The early Celtic Church in Ireland was also extremely hierarchical in the sense that top monks—arguably more than in the 'Roman' church—were very largely from top families. In a land where there was relatively little sustained authority in any form (after the druids had been vanquished in Ireland)—and probably drawing on the ancient social power of the same druids who they replaced—the Christian monks, nuns and priests exercised even more power than elsewhere in Christendom, where secular princes held more sway.

In contrast, for all its many faults—not least, its fawning on secular power, and its urbanised schism from nature—mainstream, early 'Roman' Christianity was more open to the common man (albeit literate, and excluding half of the species) and more moderate in its prescriptions . . .

However valid the reviewer's points may be (s)he misses the point of the book. The book is a search for the wholeness of Christ's universal body which has been torn asunder by schisms. We may have to join a Pentecostal church to experience signs and wonders, a Protestant church to experience committed Bible study, a Catholic church to experience the Real Presence of Christ in the sacrament administered by someone in the apostolic succession, or an Orthodox church to pray with ikons, incense, thrones and liturgy.

In the revised Study Guide edition of *Church of the Isles: a prophetic strategy for the emerging church in Britain and Ireland*, I wrote:

During the second millennium the great strands of Christ's universal church became separated. These strands include Catholic—the focus is community around Holy Communion;

Protestant—the focus is conversion around the Bible; Orthodox—the focus is the living tradition of prayer in the liturgy and the heart.[66]

I picture the universal church as a stool with these three legs. If one leg is misplaced, the stool becomes unusable.

Some critics write off this quest to weave together the strands as a wild goose chase. Maria Raikes writes that "those who look back beyond the painful separation of the Reformation in order to find their roots in a more peaceable Celtic church will only discover other divisions".[67]

Such divisions were tears in one tapestry. Catholicity was a reality. Columbanus wrote to Pope Boniface IV, "We are Catholics", and all his churches maintained the apostolic succession of deacons, priests and bishops. Celtic spirituality is scriptural. Patrick quotes from forty books of Scripture in his two short writings. Celtic spirituality is Pentecostal: prophecy and healing flourished widely in the Celtic churches. They followed the orthodox faith as defined in the councils and creeds of the world church and drew inspiration from the eastern churches of John and the Oriental churches of the desert fathers and mothers. Celtic spirituality is orthodox. They gave the Bible the highest authority and stood up to the misuse of authority in the Church (c.f. Columbanus's rebuke to the competing popes).

Is this a wild goose chase? It is true that promising ecumenical dialogues of the twentieth century have been kicked into the long grass, where they may have to wait until the Roman Catholic and Orthodox churches ordain women, which they surely will. Yet some notable people have not written off such a search, and they are surely in accord with the apostle Paul. Thomas Merton wrote in his autobiography:

> If I can unite in myself the thought and devotion of Eastern and Western Christendom, the Greek and the Latin Fathers, the Russian with the Spanish Mystics, I can prepare in myself the reunion of divided Christians . . . If we want to bring together what is divided, we cannot do so by imposing one division upon another or absorbing one tradition into another. We must contain all the divided worlds in ourselves and transcend them in Christ.[68]

Brian McLaren even dared to title one of his books *A Generous Orthodoxy: Why I Am a Missional, Evangelical, Post/Protestant, Liberal/conservative, Mystical/poetic, Biblical, Charismatic/contemplative, Fundamentalist/ Calvinist, Anabaptist/Anglican, Methodist, Catholic, Green, Incarnational, Depressed-yet-hopeful, Emergent, Unfinished Christian.*

"Having seen the spiritual and socio-political impact of a fragmented Church, I pray and hope that I may one day see a unified holistic church. I see the model of the early Celtic Church as a beacon of hope in a wilderness of disunity," a church leader wrote to me following the publication of *Exploring Celtic Spirituality.* So, the "Celtic test of catholicity" is pertinent today.

Michael Ramsey relates the nature of catholicity to the nature of Christ's incarnation.[69] Its deepest expression is in the pattern of dying and rising, as expressed in the two great sacraments of baptism and the Eucharist, and in the pattern of every member and every local community dying to self in its utter dependence upon the whole universal body of Christ (1 Corinthians 12:24–6). Control leads to schism. Service builds catholicity.

A true test of development is whether it serves the organic unity of the body in all its parts. The Scriptures, baptism, eucharist, apostolate and creeds are vindicated because they are the means by which the Gospel of God in Christ prevails over one-sided theories and perversions of the Christian life. "The structure of the church is the catholic fact. How far the Papacy expresses this main fact or distorts it is a subsequent historical question."[70]

Those with a "Celtic understanding" believe that the Roman Catholic Church itself is part of a greater whole, is on a journey, has things to learn and can only find its completeness in relationship to all members of Christ's family on earth and in heaven. They believe, in common with Michael Ramsey, that the only authentic instruments of catholicity are those that enable, rather than force, the weaker parts of the universal body of Christ to relate to the whole.

Is it too much to pray, in the spirit of Columbanus, that before long a pope will ordain women, recant for taking unilateral powers over Eastern patriarchs in 1954 and for pronouncing Anglican Orders as "null and void" in 1896, convene an eighth ecumenical council of bishops from these and other communions, and wait together on the Holy Spirit?

Michelle Brown, the Lindisfarne Gospels expert, believes that the Gospels encapsulate the truly universal, non-partisan nature of the original English church.[71] The Gospel page for Mark reflects Coptic Egypt, the Gospel page for Matthew reflects Jerusalem, that of Luke reflects Rome, and that of John reflects the East. The Gospels were crafted while the Syrian Theodore was Archbishop of Canterbury. The world's churches in all patriarchies were engaged with two issues: the date of Easter and the Monophysite issue of whether Christ was truly God even while he was on earth as Jesus. In order to address these issues, Theodore called a preparatory conference at Hatfield in 680 which culminated in the Council of Constantinople in 681. What the Gospels tell us is that they reflect all streams of the worldwide church that met at Constantinople. The church born out of the Irish and Roman missions is not only Roman, or only Coptic, or only Eastern, or only Irish, it is the one, holy, catholic and apostolic church.

To write off the Celtic tradition because of idiosyncrasies and aberrations is no more sensible than it would be to write off the Catholic Church because various self-appointed groups use the term "catholic".

Fortunately, a scholarly consensus seems to have emerged in recent years that early churches in the Celtic-speaking areas were part of Latin Christendom as a whole, honoured the role of the Bishop of Rome as in some sense the successor of the apostle Peter, and continued the ordained ministry of bishops, priests and deacons, but that there was significant variation of worship and structure within kingdoms and monastic families. Many also agree that certain traditions and practices were widely used in both the Irish and British churches, but not so much in the wider Christian world. Examples of these are the anamchara (soul friend), penitentials based on a restorative process, the dating of Easter, monastic tonsure and life-long pilgrimage.

Although local churches in Celtic lands were not immune to tribal conflicts and power struggles, the "indigenous principle" was their paradigm. This indigenous principle is vital to the credibility of future Christianity.

Although the early church in Wales was not independent, it did exercise a degree of autonomy that would have been unimaginable in later centuries. Contemporary non-Roman Catholic churches which draw on the Celtic tradition have reason to debate whether later papal claims are a legitimate part of the catholicity of the church.

This is no mere postmodern fad. Residents of Kilmacolm, west of Glasgow, will tell you that John Knox held Scotland's first Protestant communion service on the site of an ancient Celtic monastic church which is now part of the village golf course, in the mid sixteenth century. He did this to make the point that the reformed church was not a rebellious upstart: although it threw off papal powers accrued in recent centuries, it sought to be in line with the ancient church of his land.

In an audience with Cyprus's Orthodox Bishop Constantius, who represents his church on the World Council of Churches, he explained to me that Cyprus is permitted to be an autocephalous church because it was founded by an apostle (Barnabas and Paul). I reminded him that the churches outside the Roman Empire were also regarded as autocephalous. Since, as far as I am aware, no synod of the church in England formally sided with Rome's position when it unilaterally extended its powers at the time of the 1054 Orthodox/Roman Catholic schism, could the Church of England be regarded as a fellow autocephalous church? This may seem far-fetched, but not to the coarb of the Isle of Lismore. In his uniquely personal booklet Fr Niall, Coarb of St Moluag on the Isle of Lismore (through dynastic family inheritance), argues that he is still the titular abbot in the ongoing Celtic church. This role is acknowledged when he is invited to be part of the service at the consecration of the Episcopal Church of Scotland's Bishop of Argyll.[72]

Although we cannot join all the Presbyterian and Roman Catholic, Baptist, Orthodox, Episcopal and Pentecostal churches, we can allow ourselves to undergo a change of attitude and a change of worldview. We can pray with all these branches of the Church. We can regard them as our family. We can be enriched by that which is of God in their teachers and writers and iconographers and apostolic and healing initiatives. We can avoid or challenge abuse as did Columbanus. We can do what those who take vows with the international dispersed Community of Aidan and Hilda do: pledge to weave together the God-given strands in Christianity—sacramental and biblical, monastic and creation-caring, prophetic and healing—that have become separated.

CHAPTER 5

Release the power of divine womanhood

In an article in *Ecotheology* in 1998, Ian Bradley wrote: "Although it gives me no pleasure to do so, on the basis of my re-reading of many of the primary sources and also the commentaries on them by scholars I have also felt the need to retract my early endorsement of the apparently feminine-friendly character of Celtic Christianity."[73]

I don't know of any other scholar who fitted "Celtic Christianity" into modern ideas of women's equality. It was clear to me from my first days of research that the early followers of Christ in Celtic lands inherited first millennium presuppositions and were part of a patriarchal church and culture. In his article "The End of Celtic Christianity", Gilbert Markus quotes anti-women sentiments of various hermits, and points out that in Irish legal texts women were legally subject to men.[74] But the question needs to be asked, "Was there something more?" Within a patriarchal worldview, in which men were the landowners, chiefs and bishops, was there some added dimension which implicitly evokes the "Divine feminine" and the God-given role of women?

The Ireland to which the Gospel was brought had certain Gospel-friendly trends which were less prominent in the Roman Empire. Because Ireland was rural, it related to female gods (due to the importance of reproductivity and fertility in the farming and life cycles). Its first Christians were less likely to read into the biblical message an anti-feminine view of God. Second, women had more rights and roles in Irish law than in many lands, though they were not equal. Women could own and develop land in their lifetime, though upon their death it returned to the original owner. Women were capable of rising to leadership roles in tribes.

An Irish legend, put into writing by Christian monks, records that Emer, who became the wife of the hero Cu Chulainn, would only marry the man who was her equal in noble birth, beauty and wisdom. She is said to have the six gifts of womanhood: beauty, chastity, needlework, sweet speech, voice and wisdom. Her story is retold in William Butler Yeats's play *The Only Jealousy of Emer*. And in Britain visitors to Westminster still behold the iconic statue of Boudicca, the female leader of the Iceni tribe, who slew the invading Roman commander. Her late husband, King Prasutagus, had divided his estate between his daughters.

The Patrick portrayed by his earliest biographers Tírechán and Muirchu is a martial figure, who contests with druids, overthrows pagan idols, and curses kings and kingdoms. On occasion, their accounts contradict Patrick's own writings: Tírechán states that Patrick accepted gifts from female converts, although Patrick himself flatly denies this. However, the emphasis Tírechán and Muirchu placed on female converts, and in particular royal and noble women who became nuns, is thought to be a genuine insight into Patrick's work of conversion. Tírechán's account suggests that many early Patrician churches were combined with nunneries founded by Patrick's noble female converts.[75] Patrick twice refers to "monks and virgins of Christ" in his own writings.

Patrick, in his *Confession*, delights to write about "a blessed woman, Irish by birth, noble, extra-ordinarily beautiful—a true adult—whom I baptized". In contrast the neo-Platonic dualist Augustine of Hippo, in his *Confessions*, describes a woman's embrace as "sordid, filthy and horrible".

The eighth-century *Catalogue of the Saints of Ireland according to their different periods* says of the Church in Patrick's time: "They did not reject the society and services of women." Women were meant to live away from the monasteries. However, this seems to refer to the celibate male monks' cells, rather than to the entire monastic village. There are references to the *manaig* (from the Latin word *monachus*), where married men and women were expected to live as tenants outside the celibates' area, with relatively strict rules, in what Etchingham describes as a para-monastic existence.[76] Charles Stewart, in his *The Gaelic Kingdom in Scotland, Its Origin and Church*, refers to the Dewar family, who were in close connection with the monastery at Strathfillan.[77]

St Jerome, in Bethlehem, provided rules of life for well-to-do women and it seems Patrick did the same. Liam de Paor concludes that *The Life of St. Darerca, or Moninna* gives a plausible outline of the life of a female founder of the period before and after Patrick's death.[78] Before she founded a women's monastery in today's County Down, she adopted a child as her foster son, who became a bishop. She became the guest mistress under Brigid at Kildare, until she formed a women's community near Wexford under the direction of Bishop Ibar. She returned to her native province (County Louth), where 150 women joined her. There is an incidental reference in Adomnan's *Life of Columba* to a woman who wanted to separate from her husband and who hoped to join one of the women's communities in Ireland. There were clearly quite a lot.

Certain subjects deserve more extensive investigation. For example, why did the pagan Irish cult of the goddess Brigid, who "married" the divine with the land and fertility, morph into the cult of the saint Brigid and capture the imagination of the Irish with a "kitchen spirituality"?[79] Sean O Duinn OSB explores this in a chapter on "Goddesses and Gods of Ireland". Some writers surmise that whereas the early Celtic monastic churches had Scriptures and liturgies that presented God as male, folk customs in homes far removed from these blended the Christian faith with more female-friendly practices. We know that in medieval Ireland the cult of St Brigid included invocations to their spiritual mother, Mary of the Gael.

Brigid, the founder of the double monastery of women and men at Kildare, which held jurisdiction over a large part of south-west Ireland, is a historical figure. *The Annals of Ulster* give her birth as 452, and the emergence of a widespread popular cult of St Brigid is beyond question. The monastery at Kildare continued under the leadership of a woman, regarded as equal to the local bishop, for many years. When she was on her way to a church synod at Leinster, a bishop saw her coming and said: "I see the Mary of the Gael", meaning "the Peoples' Mary".

Bishop Cogitosus's *Life of St. Brigid* is the earliest life of an Irish saint we possess; scholars believe it was written not much later than 650. It is a rather unsatisfactory collection of folk tales which could have been told about all kinds of figures. However, in his prologue he writes:

This woman therefore grew in exceptional virtues and by the
fame of her good deeds drew to herself from all the provinces
of Ireland inestimable numbers of people of both sexes . . . she
established her monastery on the open expanses of the planes of
Mag Liffe (Kildare), which is the head of almost all the churches of
Ireland and holds the place of honour among all the monasteries
of the Irish. Its jurisdiction extends over the whole of the land of
Ireland, from coast to coast. Her concern was to provide for the
orderly direction of souls in all things and to care for the churches
of the many provinces which were associated with her, and she
reflected upon the fact that this could not be done without the
help of a high priest, who could consecrate churches and perform
ordinations. She summoned a famous hermit, therefore, who
excelled in all ways, and through whom God had manifested
many powers, telling him to leave his retreat and his solitary
life and to make his way to join her, so that he might govern the
church together with herself in episcopal dignity and there might
be no lack of priestly orders in her churches.[80]

How much Brigid was shaped by the existing culture of Ireland and
how much she shaped it is a matter for debate. Human flourishing and
overflowing hospitality are part of the tradition, which is kept alive by
such prayers as the following, which is often attributed to Brigid:

I would prepare a feast and be host to the great High King, with
all the company of heaven. The sustenance of pure love be in
my house, the roots of repentance in my house. Baskets of love
be mine to give, with cups of mercy for all the company. Sweet
Jesus, be there with us, with all the company of heaven. May
cheerfulness abound in the feast, the feast of the great High King,
my host for all eternity.

It was said that Brigid divided her dairy churning into twelve in honour
of the apostles, and the thirteenth in honour of Christ; this was reserved
for the poor and for guests. That tradition has been maintained in her
native Ireland, and is reflected in this Irish grace:

Bless, O Lord this food we are about to eat, and if there be any poor creature hungry or thirsty walking along the road, send them into us that we can share the food with them, just as you share your gifts with us all.

Even allowing for exaggeration, it seems clear that people in Bishop Cogitosus's time perceived Brigid to be the moral and spiritual figurehead from whose legacy the churches of Ireland were still largely shaped.

The hymn attributed to the monk Ultan (but ascribed to various others) may be one of the oldest hymns in the Irish language, written as early as the seventh century. A gloss to this adds that "Patrick is the head of the men, Brigid of the women of Ireland". It includes these words: "May Brigid guide us past crowds of devils . . . the branch with blossoms . . . The true virgin, easy to love, with great honor, the mother of Jesus . . . From her grace may Brigid rain on us."[81] The people prayed to Brigid even after her death because she was a queen of heaven.

The story, doubtless made up or embellished, that a short-sighted bishop mistakenly ordained Brigid as a bishop when receiving her vows as a nun tells us something about the hopes and desires of the Irish public. Although there was wide acceptance of male leadership, this was not cast in iron. When an old bishop was so awestruck by the aura of holy fire above Brigid that he unintentionally read the words for the consecration of a bishop over her, he told a remonstrating colleague: "I have no power in this matter; this dignity has been given by God to Brigid." This, I think, reflects the sense of proportion the Celtic church kept about ecclesiastical posts in relation to spiritual callings. I suspect this definition I found in a church encyclopaedia might sum up their attitude: "Maternity is a form of authority derived from nature, while that which is paternal is merely legal."

One of the folk traditions handed down and often repeated was as follows:

Brigid had a mind for lasting goodness that was not hidden; minding sheep and rising early; hospitality towards all folk. It is she who keeps everyone that is in straits and in dangers. It is she who puts down sicknesses; it is she who quiets the voice of the waves and the anger of the great sea. When a man or woman is filled with anger, ready to speak out in hate, they have only to call on Brigid and she will heal the home. She is the All-Healer, she is the Mother of the flocks, she is the Christ-bearer, she is the Mary of the Gael.[82]

The Brigid tradition offers an empowering image of womanhood. The imagination of the Irish was captured by goodness and flourishing mediated through a woman who was God's midwife and who towered among the "risen ones" still active among them. No wonder Alice Curtayne could write: "Saint Brigid is the midwife who brought to birth Christian Ireland."[83] *Celtic Spirituality* in *The Classics of Western Spirituality* series includes a chapter on "The Brigit Tradition, Ultan's Hymn, Cogitosus' Life and the Irish Life of Brigid".

Based on continental practice, one might expect women to be excluded or at least marginalized, but by the end of the early medieval period Clonmacnoise had at least one and possibly two satellite nunneries. In early medieval documents from Ireland and elsewhere, the craft activity most closely associated with women, including nuns, is textile production. The clearest indicator of textile work in the Irish archaeological record is the spindle whorl, an item which, along with the distaff, was considered a quintessentially female tool. No conclusive interpretation can be reached, but while Caherlehillan might have housed a community of female religious, it is safer to follow the excavator, John Sheehan, who has suggested that it was a family church with both male and female residents.[84]

Children of landowners and bards in pre-Christian Ireland were sent to foster mothers to learn life skills. In sixth-century Ireland, increasing numbers of children went to be mentored by spiritual foster mothers. These were sometimes a monastic amma or abba (an affectionate name for a spiritual mum or dad) who combined holy learning with holistic living, in a community which gave room to affections as well as devotions. St Ita was known as the foster mother of the saints of Ireland. Many children were sent to her school and community at Killeady. Ita said she wanted to hold in her hands and foster, not the children of chiefs and clerics, but Jesus, the Son of God himself. Ita's closeness to Jesus and Mary was the secret of her work. A hymn has come down to us attributed to Ita:

> It is Jesus who is nursed by me in my little hermitage. It is Jesus, with those who dwell in heaven, whom I hold against my heart each night.[85]

The seventh-century Irish Mission to the English, headed by St Aidan, began with twelve men. I suspect Aidan realized that without the spiritual foster mothers who played such a vital role in Ireland, parts of the male Anglo-Saxon psyche could never be converted. He pleaded with his friend Princess Hild to set aside her plans to join a women's monastery in Frankia and help him establish monasteries for women and men together in Northumbria.

From the seventh century in England, Frankia and Germany there was a wave of monasteries for men and women led by an abbess, usually from a royal family, inspired by the monasteries for men founded by Columbanus of Ireland. In England, these were more Saxon than Celtic, but were influenced by two Celtic sources. Oswald, king and saint, who invited Aidan's Irish mission, came to hold sway over the greater part of what is now England. He helped to bring faith to royal families in Mercia, Wessex and Essex and gave lands for monasteries for women as well as men. East Anglia's devoutly Christian King Anna had many relatives who founded double monasteries that drew inspiration from similar foundations under an abbess in Gaul such as Faremoutiers, Chelles and Joarre. These were founded earlier than any in England with the monastic boom which followed the missionary activity of Columbanus in Gaul around 600, and they adapted his Rule. Aidan invited Hilda to lead a monastery for women and men at Hartlepool and she was later put in charge of the large double monastery at Whitby.

Men were the warrior invaders who seized lands, properties and women. If, as often happened, they were killed in battle, their women and children were left to fend for themselves. The creation of stable centres of livelihood, learning and prayerfulness where each person was treated with respect was enormously attractive to women—it was a form of women's liberation.

To explain the unparalleled role of Hilda and her like we need to look at the revival of Christian community in the woman-friendly Irish style familiar to Aidan, and also note that a similar development took place more than a century later in the German church through the leadership of aristocratic women. There, thirty-six new communities for noblewomen were founded between 919 and 1024 in one diocese alone. In all three regions, England, Frankia and Germany, these developments were part of the flush of enthusiasm of new converts from paganism.

Professor Conrad Leyser, Lecturer in Medieval History at Oxford, in a study of Anglo-Saxon monasteries, thought these parallel developments prompted the question "whether there was not some underlying predicament in the pre-Christian beliefs and make-up of Franks, Saxons and Anglo-Saxons to which the endowment of nunneries furnished a welcome and eagerly sought-after solution".[86]

Christine Fell points out that we can deduce from Aldhelm's late seventh-century letters (for example, to the nuns of Barking) the wide range of their scholarly activities. He speaks of their remarkable mental disposition "roaming widely through the flowering fields of scripture . . . now scrutinising with careful application the hidden mysteries of the ancient laws . . . Now exploring wisely, the fourfold text (of the Gospels) . . . now duly rummaging through the old stories of the historians and the entries of chroniclers . . . now sagaciously inquiring into the rules of the grammarians and the teachers of experts on . . . the rules of metrics . . . " There is no reason to suppose that Whitby nuns were much different.[87]

Later royal abbesses turned their monasteries into courts. Hilda certainly received many royals, and Enfleda had Oswy buried at Whitby and, later, the remains of her father, King Edwin—it became the royal burial ground. Hilda, however, never removed her village from ordinary life. She made no distinction between a peasant and a prince, a prelate or a novice, she had space in her heart for each, believed in each and loved each. That is why uneducated people and royals alike called her mother, as did "foreigners" from outside her own kingdom of Deira.

Hilda was succeeded as abbess by the widowed queen Enfleda and then by her daughter Elfleda. Both were declared saints in their own right. Reading between the lines of Bede's sparse description of Hilda, we cannot but conclude that she exercised an extraordinary leadership role.

And why were the double monasteries for men and women in England, France and Germany, led by women and inspired by the male monasteries of Columbanus, almost unique in world Christianity, so that we had to wait a thousand years after their demise before women in such leadership positions emerged again in the Church? (The above paragraphs echo those in *Hilda of Whitby: a spirituality of now*.[88])

Iona developed a way of protecting women. Adomnan has the story of a woman speared by a man who flees to Columba for protection: the man is slain as if in answer to his prayer. A magician who kept a woman captive is compelled by Columba to free her. Iona's Abbot Adomnan promulgated his Law of Innocents amongst a gathering of Irish, Dál Riatan and Pictish notables at the Synod of Birr in 697. It is called the "Geneva Accords" of the ancient Irish, for its protection of women and non-combatants, extending the Law of Patrick (which protected monks) to civilians. The legal symposium at the Synod of Birr was prompted when Adomnan had a vision in which his mother excoriated him for not protecting the women and children of Ireland. Later, in England, Adomnan made an agreement with Saxons which protected women and children from fighting in battles. Such events set an agenda for Iona, which in time established Women's Island on the adjoining small islet. *The Martyrology of Oengus* has a commemoration "To Adomnan of Iona, whose troop is radiant, Jesus has granted the lasting liberation of the women of the Gaels".[89]

Some scholars see a connection between Iona's protection of women and its cult of the Blessed Virgin. Later editions of the *Cain Adomnan* suggest it was she who urged Adomnan to promote the Law and that he did it for the sake of Mary, mother of Jesus Christ, as if because of her solidarity with all mothers. The images of the Mother and Child on Iona's eighth-century crosses are among the oldest in these islands.

Cornwall has hundreds of villages named after saints. These include a number of women who sailed from Ireland and established a hermitage or monastic family. One of these was Ive, who gives her name to St Ives. These women were free to roam and to pioneer. St Melangell sailed across the sea and founded a hermitage in what is now Wales. She famously saved the life of a hare from hunters, and her hermitage became known as a sanctuary.

It would be mistaken to project back upon the early churches in Celtic lands the language and categories of contemporary gender equality. The women we read about in these sources were not obsessed with their rights, but they were "obsessed" with godly callings which transcended patriarchal stereotypes and offered a dimension that men could not give.

Women's monasteries can be seen as an early form of women's liberation. Monasteries for women and men led by a woman were a sign that God knows better than inherited patriarchal stereotypes. Spiritual foster mothers had a status second to none—they were the most sought-after educationalists in Ireland. The ideal of "the merciful mother"—merciful to Christians in opposing camps—makes women such as Hilda signs of the Kingdom of God.

Second millennium Celtic tradition in Scotland's highlands and islands reveals a belief that God has a mother's heart and is interested in things to do with birth and homemaking.[90]

The Wild Goose Resources Group has this liturgy:

> In the beginning God made the world
> Made it and mothered it
> Shaped it and fathered it . . .

In contemporary Celtic movements God is depicted as the Cosmic Birther. This safeguards us from divorcing God from real life.

Let us draw inspiration from empowered women who empower others, from women with merciful hearts who foster great vocations and from the mother's heart in the heart of God.

CHAPTER 6

The Bible opens windows
to God, not boxes

The criticism that Celtic Christianity is unbiblical mainly comes from a few USA fundamentalist strands. In some cases, this is because many Americans, unaware of Celtic Christianity, perceive the term "Celtic" to refer to current and ancient pagan beliefs. In other cases, it is because beliefs promulgated a few centuries ago, such as penal substitution or "the Rapture", which have been promoted as biblical, are absent in Celtic Christianity. Some conservative evangelicals read the Bible through the lens of an individualistic and dualistic culture, and therefore condemn those who make a link between personal faith and, for example, justice.

The online magazine *Reformed and Reforming: 'The truth shall make you free'* states in its 2 March 2010 edition that Celtic Christianity is not authentic Christianity:

> Modern Christians are very prone to what is fashionable in Christian circles, and most of what they accept is not authentic Christianity. By following fashions in religion, Christians become 'twee' and absurd. This applies to the fashionable following of what is called Celtic Christianity. The closest I can come to describing the overall religious content of this movement is early flawed Christianity as practiced before the Romans conquered Britain and as practiced until the papal envoy, Augustine, was sent to Canterbury in the sixth century AD to formalize Roman Catholicism throughout Britain up to the border of Pict-land.[91]

Some claim that Celtic-inspired Christians' concern for justice and for creation are unbiblical because the Bible teaches us to love not the world. Others list a set of doctrines which they claim are biblical, such as penal substitution (we deserve the death penalty for our sins, but God killed his Son instead of us), and conclude that those who do not promote them are unbiblical.

Ian Bradley makes the criticism in *Following the Celtic Way* that penal substitution does not feature in early Celtic Christianity, but scholarly consensus is that it did not feature as the main theory of atonement until the sixteenth-century European Reformation.[92] It argues that Christ, by his own sacrificial choice, was punished in the place of sinners, thus satisfying the demands of justice so God can justly forgive the sins. This doctrine has raised many questions among Christians from diverse backgrounds. Does this mean that the law of "an eye for an eye and a tooth for a tooth" is the ultimate description of God's character? How are we to understand one member of the Trinity (the Father) being wrathful towards another member of the Trinity (the Son), when they are, along with the Holy Spirit, one and the same God? Can God be truly angry with God? The theory of atonement known as Christus Victor is generally taken to be more representative of Celtic teachings, as of the early Church Fathers generally. In this understanding every aspect of Christ's life, work, death, resurrection and sending of the Spirit was part of the redeeming and atoning work of God.

Others claim that Celtic Christians ignore judgement and hell. N. D. O'Donoghue claims that the Celts lacked "that indelible sense of sinfulness and divine wrath that we find in some other Christian traditions".[93] Conservative evangelical critics claim that Celtic Christians deny the need for Christ's personal atonement for their sins, and for the finality of God's judgement. The sources contradict these charges. The *Altus Prosator*, attributed to Columba, has such sobering verses as these:

> It seems doubtful to no one that there is a hell down below . . .
> Where there is sulphurous fire burning with voracious flames;
> Where there is the screaming of men,
>> weeping and gnashing of teeth;
> where there is the groaning of Gehenna, terrible and ancient . . .

Patrick believed that because human sin resulted in his condemnation and separation from God, Christ went to "foreign parts" to help rescue lost mankind by striking it from the grasp in which the Devil held it, who was ready to mete "penal death" to the finally unrepentant.[94] The merits of Christ were felt to be vital to salvation, imputed by the Saviour to the believer (*Tripartite Life of Patrick* 2:83). They believed in a final Last Judgement, "for there will not be any sound of assembly after that".[95]

Another reason why some conservative evangelicals accuse Celtic Christianity of not being biblical is that it encourages meditation. These critics dismiss meditation as dangerous because it opens the mind to extraneous influences. David Cole, Deputy Guardian of the Community of Aidan and Hilda, dispels such misconceptions.[96] He points out that the word "meditate" or a derivative appears around twenty times in the Bible. According to the Bible, one form of meditation is to meditate upon the Scriptures: "Do not let this Book of the Law depart from your mouth; meditate on it day and night, so that you may be careful to do everything written in it" (Joshua 1:8); " . . . but his delight is in the law of the LORD, and on his word he meditates day and night" (Psalm 1:2). David Cole writes:

> To meditate upon scripture is not just simply to read the bible, but it is to savor what is there in front of you. It is to soak in the words which are living and active . . . The ancient practice of 'Lectio Divina' is a way of deeply soaking in small parts of the bible so that we can savor the spirit behind the words as well as the words themselves. The practice of Lectio Divina can be separated into 4 parts:
>
> **Read the scripture.** Do this every day. Repeatedly read the same verse, or couple of verses each day for a period of time.
>
> **Reflect on what it says.** Stop for a few moments following your reading. Think about what the words say; what they mean, and also any particular part that speaks to you. Allow, at this time, God to speak into your heart.
>
> **Respond to God.** Talk to God about what you have just read, and what thoughts you had about it. Ask him to teach you from it. You may be surprised at how many different things he says to you

over the time you spend on the same verse(s), or he may simply want to sink more deeply into your heart the same thing each day.

Relate what you have read to your life. It is no good reading the bible, even if God speaks to you through it, if you do not relate it to the way you live your life. This is not about "trying to be a good Christian", because if you do that you will only fail at it. It is about walking in a growing relationship with God and allowing him to work the truths which you have read into your everyday life.

There are also verses in the bible which show us that we can meditate on the character of God: "Within your temple, O God, we meditate on your unfailing love." (*Psalm 48:9*). To meditate upon the character of God, on his makeup, is to gain a greater and deeper understanding of who God is. We often take it for granted that we know God and that we know who he is. But as the great Christian mystics have made clear centuries ago, whatever concepts of God we have are inadequate for who he really is, or to gain a complete understanding of him (if that is ever possible), and if we simply maintain that God is only who we think he is then we have put a limit upon God and what he can do within our life.

The truth is that Celtic Christianity is steeped in the Bible. Gildas's *The Ruin of Britain*, the earliest text on the British church, quotes extensively from the Bible. St Patrick's writings overflow with biblical quotations. A beautifully illustrated booklet by Janet Craven[97] compellingly sets out how the Bible became Ireland's first book through the labours of St Patrick. She has managed to circulate this to guest houses throughout Ireland. N. J. White has counted 340 examples from forty-six books of the Bible of direct quotations or imagery in Patrick's two short writings, the *Confessio* and the *Letter to Coroticus*.[98] In his *Letter to Coroticus* Patrick writes: "The words are not mine, but of God, and the apostles and prophets, who have never lied." The Irish annals report that, in 439, Bishops Secundinus, Auxilius and Iserninus arrived in Ireland to aid St Patrick. The *Hymn of Secundinus* is found in some manuscript versions of the eleventh-century *Liber Hymnorum*. This states of Patrick: "He finds in the sacred volume the sacred treasure . . . whose seeds are seen to be the Gospel of Christ . . . "[99]

Bede's testimony to Celtic missionaries was that "they diligently followed whatever pure and devout customs that they learned in the prophets, the Gospels, and the writings of the Apostles". He commented that Aidan and his disciples "whether monks or lay folk, were required to meditate, that is, either to read the Scriptures or to learn the Psalms. That was their daily occupation wherever they went".[100]

A primary task in the large monastic settlements was to copy the texts of the Bible in a scriptorium and to memorize and chant psalms and other texts in chapel. Cummean, in his penitentiary, c. 650, writes: "He who takes up any novelty outside the Scriptures such as might lead to heresy, shall be sent away . . . "

The Bible remains a fundamental element of Celtic Christianity. Ron Ferguson makes clear that George MacLeod himself became critical of the Iona Community towards the end of his life. He gathered people to his manse to make up for the Community's neglect of biblical and Pentecostal elements in his message.[101]

So, if early Celtic Christians were so steeped in the Bible, why do certain Christians make this accusation that they are unbiblical? This issue brings us to the human need to make constructs, or to put God in a box. Each of us inherits a worldview derived from our upbringing, our tribe or the church through which we are converted. The writers and scribes of Scriptures fit divine inspirations into their inherited constructs. Only if we allow the living Word behind the words to speak through our constructs, transforming them in the process, do we save ourselves from being idolaters in the guise of Bible Christians.

One example of using the Bible to box God in is to apply the injunction to "love not the world" as an excuse for abdicating responsibility for this world. 1 John 2:15–16 says: "Do not love the world or anything in the world. If anyone loves the world, love for the Father is not in them. For everything in the world—the lust of the flesh, the lust of the eyes, and the pride of life—comes not from the Father but from the world." Yet John 3:16 begins, "For God so loved the world . . . ." So, God loves the world, but we are not supposed to? Why the apparent contradiction?

In the Bible, the term "world" can refer to the earth and physical universe (Hebrews 1:2; John 13:1), or to the corrupt human value system that opposes God (Matthew 18:7; John 15:19; 1 John 4:5). When we are told not to love the world, the Bible is referring to the world's corrupt value system. Satan is the god of this world, and he has his own value system contrary to God's (2 Corinthians 4:4). 1 John 2:16 details exactly what Satan's system promotes: the lust of the flesh, the lust of the eyes, and the boastful pride of life. Every sin imaginable can be summed up in those three evils; envy, adultery, pride, lying, selfishness and more spring from those three roots. The world is what we leave when we come to Christ. Isaiah 55:7 says that coming to God involves a forsaking of our own ways and thoughts.

Celtic glossators do not put God in a box. They are open to different ways of reflecting on Scripture. They treat the texts as windows, not as boxes.

What methods of interpretation did the early Celtic churches adopt? They were not hidebound. They used literal, allegorical and visionary methods. John Scotus Eriugena wrote in his *Division of Nature* (866): "For there are many ways, indeed an infinite number, of interpreting the Scriptures, just as in one and the same feather of a peacock and even in the same small portion of the feather, we see a marvelously beautiful variety of innumerable colors."

However, it seems likely that their earliest model was Cassian (360–435). He advised his disciples to set aside commentators, to devote their time to prayer, fasting and meditation so as to reach an understanding of the Scriptures, promising them that God would reveal to them in their dreams the meaning of the passages they had reflected upon. Cassian identified four ways in which the Bible could be understood: the literal, the symbolic, the ethical and the mystical. The literal reads the texts in their "natural" or "historical" sense, because it deals with actual events, actual people and actual statements. Another way to read biblical texts is on a deeper, more symbolic level. This was often known as the allegorical or typological method. The Bible itself includes a clear example of this. The apostle Paul wrote that the story about Abraham and his two wives, Hagar and Sarah, could be read allegorically. He interpreted it to refer to the difficult relationship between Jewish people and Christians of his time

(Galatians 4:22–31). A third way of interpreting the Bible is to look for an "ethical" meaning. This is sometimes known as the moral or tropological sense. It involves reading between the lines of a Bible passage or verse to see how it applies to daily life. 1 Corinthians 9 in the New Testament contains an example of midrash. The apostle Paul quotes a saying from the Old Testament (9:9, 10) about oxen and then "explains" what the text actually implied on an ethical level (i.e. that apostles have the right to financial support). A fourth kind of interpretation finds mystical or eschatological meaning within Bible texts. Mystical in this sense usually involves interpreting texts to reveal something about the future. For example, the book of Revelation uses the word "Jerusalem" to refer to the heavenly future of Christians (Revelation 21:2). Therefore, wherever some interpreters found the word Jerusalem elsewhere in the Bible, they concluded that it also had something to say about heaven.[102]

In Britain, Samson (d. 565) had such an acute desire to understand deeper meanings of the Scriptures that if he or his teacher (Illtud, the learned leader of the great monastic school at Llantwit Major) came across a doubtful point, even though they had carefully studied all the books of the Old and New Testaments, Samson undertook fasts and vigils until God's understanding broke through. He was praying at nearly midnight when a heavenly light appeared and a voice spoke out of the light: "Do not trouble yourself any further on this, God's chosen one, for in future whatever you ask God for in prayer and fasting you will obtain." Then Samson returned quite happy to his cell and told Illtud, his teacher, all he had seen and heard.[103]

The early seventh-century elegiac poem *Amra Choluim Chille*, ascribed to Dallán Forgaill (derived from an annotated redaction that was made in the beginning of the eleventh century), is accompanied by extensive commentary in Middle Irish. Columba was believed by his biographer to have had a system of biblical interpretation on the following lines:

> He divided a division with figures, between the books of the law,
> i.e. he divided a division with allegorizing between the books of
> reading or of Lex, i.e. of the Law of each, the Old Law and the New
> Testament, i.e. he used to distinguish history (stair) and sense
> (sian), morality (morail) and mystical interpretation (anogaig).[104]

Most accusations that Celtic Christianity is not biblical come from Christians who view everything through an individualistic lens. It is true that neither Celtic nor any ancient societies had fallen prey to the false over-individualism which afflicts today's Western societies and churches. The early churches in Celtic-speaking lands were influenced by Athanasius. In his famous work *On the Incarnation of the Word of God* Athanasius expounds how in Christ's incarnation God unites himself with all humanity and all creation because, although it is fragmented and has pulled away from its divine source, it is all God's. So, I cannot be saved as a disconnected entity.

A this-worldly spirituality breathes through the Bible. James Mackey writes in the preface to *Celtic Spirituality* (Paulist Press):

> The Divine Word, which continuously creates the world, takes human form in Jesus of Nazareth who, as life-giving spirit, forms his extended body from fellow-humans down the ages. It is to this body that the physical world itself looks for a like liberation from evil and finitude, the liberations of the sons of God, until in the eschaton all together share eternal fulfilment in the new heaven-and-earth. It is this biblical spirituality that breathes through Celtic spirituality, which has never fallen prey to the separation of the individual from the rest of life. So when I accept Jesus, I see myself as the first fruits of a new creation.

The cross of Christ is central to all biblical expressions of Christianity, including the Celtic. For some conservative evangelicals, the cross is something God did for me, and if I ask, I will escape the punishment I deserve for my sins and go to heaven. The cross is about Christ and me. The Celtic understanding of the cross includes that truth, but it connects it to my fellow humans and to the universe. In response to requests I produced the followed Celtic Cross Prayer Card:

> The Cross shape: Jesus, God's eternal and human Son was crucified on a cross of wood cut from a tree so that whoever puts their trust in him should not die in their sins but have everlasting life. Jesus calls us to take up our cross and follow him daily.

The Circle: The circle is a universal, inclusive sign. In psychology, the circle is a primal symbol of wholeness. Jesus did not die just to give certain believers a passport to heaven; his total self-giving transforms every aspect of our lives, and of the cosmos: "As in Adam all die, so in Christ shall all be made alive" (1 Corinthians 15:22). Our inner lives are a continent, parts of which have still to be evangelized. These, and areas of society that are alienated from good and God, are to be transformed, not neglected. Nothing is outside God's love.

The Cross Base: This is the broadest part. The large stone Celtic crosses stand firm in the soil. God wants to root us in the soil of creation and sanctity, to make us earthy and earthed Christians, to be real and practical, to find God in our work and in the earth, which is our home.

The Top of the Cross: This narrows but reaches, as it were, into heaven. It points us to the world of adoration, mystical prayer, visions, thin places, and the final passage from this life. We make time to be alone with God, to become aware of the saints and angels and to chant and sing with them—to experience "heaven in the ordinary things of life".

The Cross Arms: The Divine Christ eternally stretches out his arms in suffering love—that is why the human Christ could do it for one day nailed to the arms of the Cross. The right arm signifies forgiveness towards all. The left arm pictures service of all. The two cross beams also speak of symmetry—one side balances the other. We seek a balance, a rhythm between input and output, work and prayer, suffering and celebration, withdrawal and outreach.

Spaces: The four spaces in the Cross are in a sense nothing, but the other features would be lost without them. God designs spaces for us.

The Heart: In the middle is the heart of it all. This is not only the heart of the piece of wood, it represents the heart of God—the place where the Three Loves of the Trinity commune in an eternal dance and hospitably invite us in.

The Tree: The apostles Peter and Paul describe the Cross as a tree—the two cross beams may have been cut from the same tree (Acts 5:30; 10:39; 13:29; 1 Peter 2:24). This image flowered in the imagination of people such as Poitiers's hymn-writing Bishop Venantius Fortunatus ("faithful cross above all other, one and only noble tree . . . ") and in other Celtic lands. The Cross becomes the Tree of Death, linked to Eden's tree of human disobedience in the Bible's first book (Genesis 3), that becomes the Tree of Life, linked to the ultimate healing of nations tree depicted in the Bible's last book (Revelation 22). The Cross, with Christ no longer there because He has risen from death, becomes the Tree of Life.

Celtic Christianity does challenge each person to be born again, but its biblical message to over-individualistic conservative evangelical critics is: "Be born again as a first fruits of God's new creation."

In her chapter on "The Role of the Scriptures", Leslie Hardinge mines many glosses in tracts on Scripture by Celtic teachers.[105] Many of these come from *Thesaurus Palaeohibernicus*.[106] Hardinge compares the thousands of Irish glosses written between the lines of biblical manuscripts or commentaries to the midrash written by Jewish scholars on the canonical text.

A study of these glosses suggests that the variety of forms of interpretation was widespread in the Celtic Church. On the back of such material *The Celtic Bible Commentary*, edited by Kenneth McIntosh, has been launched by Anamchara Books USA. He writes of the first method: "Reading the Bible as grounded in time and space is a practice with perennial value because God has addressed humanity through the medium of the physical world: the Bible has specific historical and geographical contexts."

A number of the legal texts may be categorized together on account of related authorship. The largest such grouping is the *Senchas Már*, a collection of at least forty-seven separate tracts compiled into a single group sometime in the eighth century, though individual tracts vary in date. These tracts are almost certainly written by a variety of authors. A number of laws were grouped into triads. The prologue ascribes the authorship of the book to a committee of nine appointed by St Patrick to revise the laws. It was composed of three kings, three bishops and three professors of literature, poetry and law. Chief among the latter was Dubthach. It became his duty to give a historical retrospect, and in doing so he exhibited:

> all the judgments of true nature which the Holy Ghost had spoken from the first occupation of this island down to the reception of the faith. What did not clash with the word of God in the written law and in the New Testament and with the consciences of believers was confirmed in the laws of the brehons by Patrick and by the ecclesiastics and chieftains of Ireland. This is the Senchus Mor.[107]

The Irish Brehon laws incorporate many of the Mosaic laws. The Irish understood that God was calling them to become a country organized according to laws revealed by God, but these enhanced, rather than obliterated, their existing laws. Hardinge concludes: "The legislation of Moses pervaded social, economic, and legal relationships to an extent seldom seen in the history of other branches of the Church." It was only after the Viking invasions that more stress was placed upon tradition than upon the Bible.

Increasing numbers of committed evangelicals lose their faith because they are open-minded, and the internet introduces them to alternative explanations for created life and religious beliefs. They were brought up with a version of religion that made them prisoner of a particular construct. In their integrity they dispense with that construct. Too many Christians become trapped in a narrow, monochrome construct which, often unknowingly, they superimpose upon the text of Scripture. At the other extreme, very liberal Christians may de-mythologize all Scripture so much that the living God is not invited into the process. The value of the Celtic approach is that it has many strings to its bow. It does not put God into boxes. It does open windows to God.

Millennials who give up religion do not give up exploring. Expressions of inner pilgrimage and new monasticism, inspired by the Celtic spirit, which commit us to life-long exploring are more likely to meet their need.

These do not offer a finished list of what others have seen: they offer us a new way of seeing.

The Bible is agreed by the universal church to be the canonical text of the Church. Whereas for Muslims the Word of God is the Book (the Qur'an), for the universal church the Word of God is a Person (Christ). Every human writer, including those who wrote or edited the thousands of writings included in the Bible, composes their words through the lens of a mental construct which they receive from their upbringing, tribe/society and reflection. It is the belief of mainstream, and certainly Celtic, Christians that the living Word interacts with the biblical texts. The task of the prayerful reader is to discern what gleam of light God is imparting to a particular person or group, and how we may learn from this in our different circumstances.

CHAPTER 7

Our world thirsts to draw from ancient well-springs

A common criticism is that sources for early Celtic Christianity are too fragmentary to build anything on. It is, of course, true that source materials for the early Christian centuries in Celtic lands are fewer than sources for later periods, when writings of historians and recordists increased and were better preserved. They are not, however, insubstantial, and in the years since I wrote *Exploring Celtic Spirituality* a huge amount of work has been done to collect, compare, annotate, translate or re-publish previously inaccessible documents. Ongoing archaeological digs continue to bring new information to light and ancient pilgrim places and routes are being restored.

The call of prophets such as Jeremiah to "look for the ancient routes . . . set up landmarks, and return to me by the road by which you travelled here" (Jeremiah 6:16; 31:21) has abiding validity.

Columbia University first published James F. Kenney's *Sources for the Early History of Ireland (Ecclesiastical)* in 1929. This gives details of 659 source documents. In 1966, the eminent scholar Ludwig Bieler edited a revised edition of *The Irish Penitentials* (Dublin: Institute for Advanced Studies, 1975). Four Courts Press, Dublin, which has kept this in print, has developed a substantial catalogue of serious works on Celtic Studies.[108] Liam de Paor's *Saint Patrick's World* (Four Courts Press, 1993) provides a good selection of source documents. *The Celtic Monk: Rules & Writings of Early Irish Monks* by Uinseann O. Maidin (Cistercian Publications c/o Liturgical Press, 1996) provides us with several eighth-century Irish Rules which do include some practical guidance, but they do not set out an ordered basis for community. The Rule, Sermons and Letters of Columbanus are readily available in various editions.

As regards sources for Christianity in early Britain, Gildas's *The Ruin of Britain and Other Works*, translated by Michael Winterbottom in *History from the Sources* (Phillimore, London and Chichester, 1978), was written in the sixth century and provides some material contained in his Jeremiah-like tirade against corruption in the post-Roman rump of a church. *The Life of St Samson of Dol*, edited by Thomas Taylor (Llanerch, 1991), is thought to have been written by Samson's nephew in the seventh century and is clearly based on earlier materials. Bede's *Ecclesiastical History of the English People* (Oxford University Press, written about 731), is the chief solid history, albeit written through a Roman lens. Bede wrote many other books, including Bible commentaries and both a prose and poetic *Life of Saint Cuthbert*. An anonymous monk at Lindisfarne also wrote a *Life of Saint Cuthbert* which Bede draws from. Nennius's *The History of the Britons* (Kessinger Publishing, 2004) was written about 828 and provides anecdotal, but not historically verified, information. Haddan and Stubbs's *Councils and Ecclesiastical Documents Relating to Great Britain and Ireland* (4 vols, Oxford University Press, 1869–78) begins with the third century.

Oliver Davies, in *Celtic Spirituality* (Paulist Press, 1999), lists numerous sources from the classic Celtic period under these headings: Hagiography, Monastic, Poetry, Devotional, Liturgy, Apocrypha, Exegesis, Homilies and Theology. Boydell and Brewer, at Ipswich, continues to publish major works on Celtic Studies in Britain and Ireland. Detailed academic analyses of numerous hagiographies pour off university and other presses (such as *Celtic Hagiography and Saints' Cults*[109]). There is a large corpus of hagiography. These stories have been collected by various writers and editors. (For example, G. H. Doble's *Cornish Saints* and *Welsh Saints* series; *The Lives of the British Saints: The Saints of Wales and Cornwall and Such Irish Saints As Have Dedications in Britain* by S. Baring-Gould and John Fisher (Classic Reprint, Forgotten Books, 2012)).

Bede informs us that Aidan brought the Rule of Columba to the Anglo-Saxons. Since this was not written down, we can only intuit from sayings, practices and qualities of Columba as recorded by Adomnan something of the Iona way of life that Aidan continued in Northumbria.

We know that Aidan himself was both gentle and culture-friendly, so it is very likely that Aidan's Rule blended in these characteristics. Scholars generally assume that Hilda's Rule for men and women at Whitby blended Aidan's Rule with that of Columbanus, which influenced her sister's monastery at Chelles, in Gaul, and perhaps also that of Benedict.

Archaeological research has increased by leaps and bounds in recent years. Even as I write, an archaeological dig to examine the remains of the Celtic monastery at Fortingall, Scotland, is under way. At some sites, such as Whithorn, ongoing archaeological and study centres have been established.[110]

A growing number of universities in Britain, Ireland, North America and elsewhere have established or further developed Celtic Studies departments, often with their own publications and libraries that stock learned journals. To name but a few: the universities of Cork, Dublin, Edinburgh, Glasgow, Manchester, Sydney (Australia) and Wales. Within the University of Toronto, St Michael's College provides Celtic and Medieval Studies. In the USA, Harvard University has a Department of Celtic Languages and Literature and the University of California offers Berkeley Celtic Studies. Although the primary focus of studies in such universities as Cambridge (UK) and Harvard may not be Christianity as such, writings by Christians play a significant part.

Celtic Studies in universities show fresh promise. In 2019, Oxford University restored its Chair of Celtic Studies in perpetuity. Professor Thomas Charles-Edwards, who served from 1997–2011, had not been replaced. This is an interdisciplinary subject, touching on history, archaeology, English, linguistics, and medieval and modern languages. Often described as "the Classics of the British Isles", Celtic Studies provides its students with a crucial understanding of the cultural and linguistic formation not only of Britain and Ireland, but of Europe as a whole.

Daniel Taylor, a fourth-year modern languages (German and Celtic) student at Jesus College, said:

> The wealth of literature and linguistic complexity makes the
> subject not only personally rewarding, but also means there
> is so much more work to be done for us to understand these

Celtic texts as much as we understand the medieval literatures of Germany, Italy and France, and the transmission of ideas between these areas.[111]

Criticisms that the sources of, say, Benedictine spirituality are too fragmentary to build much upon are seldom heard. Presumably, this is because there is one foundational document, The Rule of Benedict. The earliest Rules of Celtic monasteries were rooted in the life and teaching of the founder; only later were they written down. Columbanus is an exception, but his Rule (though it probably reflected the Rule of Bangor, where Columbanus trained) was written for pioneer missionary recruits to the continent of Europe who were so intoxicated with God that they volunteered to undergo exertions and disciplines that could not be sustained in more settled conditions. Like other Irish Rules, that of Columbanus forms a "Mirror of Perfection" for guidance in the spiritual life rather than practical regulations for the good organization of a monastery.

I sometimes meet pilgrims who say they are attracted to Celtic Christianity, but it cannot compete with, say, Ignatian Spirituality centres, because they have systematized courses in spiritual discernment. This is a half-truth. Much "Ignatian Spirituality" has been built up by Jesuits who combine Jungian and other modern disciplines with St Ignatius Loyola's written sources in their spiritual formation programmes. In fact, Pelagius taught the basics of spiritual discernment in a schema just as clear and ordered as did Ignatius. I set this out in chapter six of *Soulfriendship*.[112]

Before critics banish Celtic Christianity to a never-never land, they might also do well to consider the continuity of place. Admittedly, most of the great Celtic foundations are no longer living communities, and most people in the world need to link with thin places in their own countries that have little connection with those in lands where a Celtic language is spoken—nevertheless there remain a few places where the Celtic heritage is a lived spirituality. Glendalough in Ireland, Iona in Scotland, St David's in Wales and Lindisfarne in England are but four examples. Many come to seek a Presence and to pray at Glendalough. Here, the lake in which Kevin prayed daily, his cell and later churches built on the "monastic city" are preserved. Fr Michael Rodgers and others offer retreats and act as pilgrim guides. The Iona Community sustains creative daily worship in Iona Abbey and hosts community weeks, retreats and working parties at its Abbey Accommodation and MacLeod Centre. The Church in Wales cathedral draws many worshippers to the site of St David's main monastery. The Holy Island of Lindisfarne has two retreat houses, daily worship in the parish church, the St Cuthbert's Centre, the Lindisfarne Gospels Centre and the priory museum. One of the retreat houses is hosted by the Community of Aidan and Hilda, which also has a Celtic Studies library. Celtic Christianity is earthed.

Praying and making pilgrimage in places made holy by Celtic saints are also fast reviving practices which enable many to reconnect with "ancient paths". The Camino in Celtic Galicia, Spain, is world-famous. Ireland now has its own Camino. Five of its twelve Pilgrim Paths, each named after a local saint, are fully signed and certificated and form the Camino.[113] The Scottish Pilgrim Routes Forum gives details of pilgrim ways that criss-cross Scotland, including Three Saints Way, Whithorn Way, St Cuthbert's Way, Kentigern Way, Forth to Farne and the Fife Pilgrim Way. The North Wales Pilgrim Way is a 132-mile walk from Basingwerk to Bardsey. St David's to Holywell. The British Pilgrimage Trust includes pilgrim routes from Cornwall to Canterbury, the English Midlands (Two Saints Way) to Durham, and in the Isle of Man. There are now pilgrim routes in the Orkneys and in the Shetlands.

The Celtic crosses in the market towns of both Ireland and Britain stand as memory stones of a faith that once was ablaze with the love of God, and as way marks, pointing us to return to the Cross, our Way of Life. Websites such as <https://www.claddaghdesign.com/history/a-guide-to-irish-high-crosses/> give a bird's eye view. *The Early Christian Monuments of Scotland* (two-volume set) by J. Romilly Allen and Joseph Anderson (Angus: The Pinkfoot Press, 1993) remains a definitive work.

Today, the media serve a similar purpose to those stones, but they too often communicate a godless message. The importance of signs that stand for Christ amidst modern idolatries cannot be underestimated.

Isaac reopened the wells that had been dug in the time of his father Abraham (Genesis 26:18). This has become a timeless metaphor for spiritual re-mining and renewal. Wells are only a small part of a landscape. They can become disused and overlaid. But when a nation's entire water supply becomes polluted, some wells that still have pure water can be reactivated.

Edwin Muir's poem "Transfiguration" expresses this truth:

> So from the ground we felt that virtue branch
> Through all our veins till we were whole, our wrists
> As fresh and pure as water from a well,
> Our hands made new to handle holy things,
> The source of all our seeing rinsed and cleansed
> Till earth and light and water entering there
> Gave back to us the clear unfallen world.

Recovery of memory is a valid and necessary precursor to transfiguration.

Our memory of our past, and our sense of rootedness, have been lost. This has brought alienation, which destroys the unity of humanity; individualism, which destroys community; the divorce of rights from responsibilities; and the abuse of the created world.

Tahg Jonathan writes about the important work of remembering in an age of forgetfulness. Miroslav Volf points out that it is important to remember rightly. There is the face of Christ to our remembering; Love is the alignment and enables a coherence.[114]

St Aidan's Trust, the forerunner to the Community of Aidan and Hilda, committed itself to "restore—the memory, landmarks, witness and experience of the Celtic Church in ways that relate to God's purposes today".

Memory makes possible transfiguration. This is a key word in Arnold Toynbee's multi-volume *A Study of History* (Oxford University Press). He describes different ways of responding to history in what he calls a declining and frustrated civilization. Commenting on these, Archbishop Michael Ramsey stated:

> The first he calls archaism, and by that he means an attempt to put the clock back and to reconstruct some state of affairs which had previously existed. Another attitude he calls futurism, and by that he means to despair of the existing world order and to try to force our way forward to some totally new order unrelated

to it, so unrelated to it, that it can only be brought about by violence. The third attitude he calls detachment, but as there is a kind of detachment quite different from what he means, he would have done better to have called it escapism, for by this attitude, he means despairing of the world order and retreating from it into a kind of zone of spirituality apart from the world and its troubles. Rejecting these three attitudes as unsatisfactory, archaism, futurism and detachment, Toynbee says the true attitude that makes sense is transfiguration, and he describes transfiguration thus: 'To accept the situation just as it is and to carry it into a larger context which makes sense of it and gives the power to grapple with it'. . . . I think the words have immense suggestiveness for us Christians . . . That larger context is Jesus crucified and risen, and we are called, again and again, to be lifting human situations into that context and finding that in that context new and exciting things begin to happen to the situations, and to us who are confronting them.[115]

"God has not left us without a witness" (Acts 14:17). The twenty-five chapters in my *Exploring Celtic Spirituality* each explore an element in Celtic Christianity. Intuition and reflection play a part. But they mostly draw from early as well as later sources which I still believe stand scrutiny. They are not unique, but they are not overlaid. They are like pure wellsprings. There is much more water elsewhere, but we would be foolish to ignore these precious and God-given sources.

CHAPTER 8

To know the beauty of our origins inspires us to live for good

Some critics reject Celtic Christianity as Pelagian and therefore as heretical. Pelagius was the earliest world-famous theologian from Celtic lands but spent most of his teaching ministry in Rome and Africa. Pelagius is his Latin name; the Welsh know him as St Morgan. He had a wrestler's frame and a monk's way of life. Although many of his works have been lost, we have his "Commentary on Paul's Letters to the Romans",[116] some of his "Letters of Spiritual Direction",[117] and extracts from other works on subjects such as nature and the Trinity. He was widely esteemed as a man of great holiness and learning, steeped in the teachings of the post-apostolic Fathers of the Church. He and Augustine at first spoke highly of one another but then became uneasy. Pelagius became concerned lest Augustine's new formulation of a doctrine of original sin led to fatalism and moral laxity. Augustine, who as a young man had embraced the Manichean heresy that matter is intrinsically evil and mind is intrinsically good, became concerned lest Pelagius's emphasis on human responsibility undermined the doctrines of original sin and that God predestined all things. Augustine played politics. He persuaded the Roman Emperor to ask local church councils in the West to condemn Pelagius as a heretic. The Eastern Church, which never fell prey to the dualistic theology of the Western Church, never condemned Pelagius, nor did any council of the universal church. These issues are explored by Robert F. Evans.[118]

We need to consider two issues: Is Celtic Christianity Pelagian and was Pelagius heretical?

Is Celtic Christianity Pelagian? The texts that have come down to us give him very little recognition as a shaper of Irish or British faith patterns. Gilbert Markus, in his article "The End of Celtic Christianity", claims that "the only evidence for Pelagianism among Celtic Christians is the fact that Irish scholars continued to use Pelagius' commentaries on Paul's epistles. But . . . churches elsewhere also used the commentaries. Secondly, Pelagius' commentaries on Paul are entirely orthodox . . . ."[119]

Markus overlooks, however, that the Synod of Troyes in 429 sent Bishop Germanus on two missions to try and stamp out Pelagianism, which it saw as a peculiarly British disease. There is no doubt that what continental authorities branded as "Pelagianism" took root widely in Britain, nor that the two missions of Bishop Germanus to root it out were part of attempts by Roman secular and ecclesiastical leaders to control Britain now that the Roman troops had left, that the Britons had refused to support Constantine, and factions in the Romano-British leadership increased. The *Vita Germani* expands on Germanus's two visits to Britain, the first in 429 and a supposed second visit (which Prosper does not mention) some years later.[120]

Pelagius was either a British Celt by birth or perhaps the product of an Irish community living in Wales.[121] Much of what Pelagius argued in his ascetical rather than his theological writings can be understood as the cry of indignation of an uncompromising rural monastic at the fashionable Christianity of Rome during the onset of a new liberal age. To this extent at least Pelagius belongs to the Celtic world, on the margins of Europe and deeply imbued with early monastic ideals.

Ian Bradley writes that "the overriding impression given" (of early Celtic monastic sources including Pelagius) "is of puritanical perfectionism which encouraged a kind of spiritual elitism. It presents a forbidding and not altogether attractive picture."[122] The saying "beauty is in the eye of the beholder" expresses the fact that not all people have the same opinions about what is attractive. Bradley's conclusion evades the question of the value of models, the thrill of being all out, and the beauty of walking hand in hand with God. Some would argue that Pelagius preaches no more and no less than John Wesley, who urged Christians, in the words of Jesus, to "be perfect as your Father in heaven is perfect" (Matthew 5:48).

Folklore has sometimes branded the British as incorrigibly Pelagian, in the sense that they are more likely to find God in a garden than in the sacraments of the Church. Others claim that many Celtic enthusiasts see the good side of life and gloss over the dark side, and they call this, without foundation, Pelagian.

We might conclude that although Celtic Christianity is not the same as Pelagianism, and those who reject Pelagius's teachings may still identify with Celtic Christianity, Pelagius's teachings are a strand within it. He was part of the ascetic, monastic movement that spread through the British and Irish Isles from North Africa.

J. Philip Newell firmly allies Pelagius to the Celtic tradition.[123] He distinguishes between what he calls the Celtic and the Mediterranean traditions. Celtic spirituality is marked by the belief that what is deepest in us is the image of God. Sin has distorted and obscured that image but not erased it. The Mediterranean tradition, on the other hand, in its doctrine of original sin has taught that what is deepest in us is our sinfulness. This has given rise to a tendency to define ourselves in terms of the ugliness of our sin instead of the beauty of our origins. This makes a difference to the way we see other people. It undergirds the universal value of the sanctity of all human life.

The second question is, was Pelagius heretical? In most first millennium writings that come from the Western Church, under the influence of Augustine, he was so presented. But as time has gone by, more of his writings have come to prominence, and more sifting and reflection has taken place.[124]

There is a growing consensus that Pelagius was orthodox in faith as well as holy in his life. He would stroll through Rome's streets exhorting people, including the poor and women, to follow the ways of Christ. He became a noted spiritual advisor to aristocratic women and a number of his letters of spiritual direction, whose orthodoxy is not questioned, have been preserved.[125] He was appalled by the moral laxity of many Christians, and even more appalled that their behaviour seemed to be buttressed by the teachings of Augustine and Jerome. He chastised the wealthy and powerful, including Emperor Honorius, for their abuses of property and privilege, exhorting them to the Christian virtues of mercy and charity. His passion was that people imitated the ways of Christ rather than ticked off a list of doctrines about Him. He wrote:

You will realize that doctrines are inventions of the human mind, as it tried to penetrate the mystery of God. You will realize that Scripture itself is the work of human minds, recording the example and teaching of Jesus. Thus it is not what you believe that matters; it is how you respond with your heart and your actions. It is not believing in Christ that matters; it is becoming like him.

Augustine, however, thought that Pelagius minimized the hold of sin, and the need for God's grace. In 415, Augustine wrote his work *On Nature and Grace* in response to Pelagius's work *On Nature*. He managed to persuade a local church council to condemn him as a heretic, though this was later rescinded.

In some quarters, both Roman Catholic and Reformed, Augustine is looked upon as the father of Western Christianity. In recent years increasing numbers of theologians have reconsidered this opinion. They see in Augustine's writings the seeds of a split in the holistic nature of Christianity, which underlie the political split between the Western and Eastern churches. Augustine formulated a doctrine of original sin whereby Adam's sin and guilt are transmitted by procreation to all human beings. Augustine buttressed this teaching by references to a number of the early church fathers. Pelagius, in his work *On Nature*, which is now lost, taught that the Creator has implanted in humans the capacity to avoid sin, as a gift of grace. He, too, draws from a range of early church fathers to support this teaching.[126]

Augustine promulgated the doctrines of original sin as a congenital disease passed on at birth and of predestination and election by God's grace. Morgan believed such doctrines were un-Scriptural and were not supported by the writings of the early church fathers. One of his arguments against this doctrine was that if the sin of Adam harms even infants who are not guilty of the original sin, then the offspring of two baptized parents can scarcely inherit what their parents no longer possess. Morgan taught that Adam's sin set a habit which increasingly others imitated, but that there were always some people who continued to walk with God, such as Enoch and Noah.

Augustine thought that Pelagius undermined his doctrine of God's predestined grace—some were the elect and some were the damned eternally. Pelagius taught that God's grace was implanted in humans from their creation in their capacity to respond to God, and in the law given through Moses, as well as through the work of Christ incarnate on earth. God's grace, however, does not annul free will. He speculated that Augustine's theology was laced with his previous Manichaeism—which taught a radical dualism between spirit and matter, and a hierarchical division between the elect and the unsaved. Morgan believed that these were partly responsible for the perpetuation of abuses in Rome. Morgan thought they contributed to a Christian fatalism which denied human responsibility for sin and granted divine sanction to an unaccountable hierarchical society.

Jerome was considered the greatest of Latin Church teachers. Yet he was known to be sarcastic, impatient, arrogant, abrasive and egotistical in dealing with other Christians. Many, including Morgan, reacted negatively to Jerome's personal abuse and libels. Augustine and Jerome combined to attack Pelagius and have local church councils condemn him for heresy. They persuaded Emperor Honorius, whom Pelagius had rebuked, to join their side. Pelagius was acquitted of heresy in a June 415 Jerusalem synod, and at a council in Lydda. So dissatisfied Augustinians convened two of their own local councils in 416 at Carthage and Milevum, where they condemned Pelagius, who was not present to defend himself. The Augustinians persuaded Pope Innocent to issue a conditional condemnation of Morgan on 27 January 417, but the pope died on March 12 and was replaced by Pope Zosimus I on March 18. Zosimus was an Eastern Christian who decided to re-examine the case, calling for a synod at the Basilica of St Clement in Rome. Morgan was unable to attend but sent a Confession of Faith. Zosimus was favourably impressed with Morgan's defence and proclaimed that Morgan was totally orthodox and catholic and that he was a man of unconditional faith. Zosimus went on to say that Morgan had for many years been outstanding in good works and in service to God; he was theologically sound and never left the catholic faith. The conditional condemnation was effectively overturned. On 21 September 417, Zosimus advised the African Church (which included Augustine's diocese of Carthage): "Love peace, prize love, strive after harmony. For it is written: Love thy neighbour as thyself." He upbraided them for their discord in the Church and ordered them to cease their disruptions.

Three councils had declared Pelagius innocent of heresy. Disobedient, the Augustinians appealed to the Roman Emperor Honorius, a target of Morgan's exhortations against the abuses of wealth and power, who willingly came to their assistance. He instructed Zosimus to condemn Pelagius as a heretic.

Within the context of personalities and politics (ecclesiastical and secular) it appears that the Augustinian campaign against Morgan was only part of a developing conflict between the West and the East over the primacy of Rome and the dominance of Latin theology over the whole Church. Not so curiously, St Morgan was condemned by Western, pro-Augustinian synods and the Roman Emperor while exonerated by Eastern, non-Augustinian synods and a pope of Eastern origin. It has been frequently commented that if Morgan had been born in the East there never would have been a controversy. As it is, no canon of any ecumenical council of the undivided Church ever condemned Morgan of heresy, and the Orthodox Church has not adopted Augustine's teaching about original sin.

For Morgan, Christianity was not an abstract system of thought but a concrete way of life. Unlike Augustinianism, with its grounding in neo-Platonic philosophy and Manichean religion, Morgan's theology is grounded predominantly in the Holy Scriptures and the early church fathers. Morgan believed that all people can be saved if they choose to accept the saving grace of Christ through baptism. They are not saved by their own merits, but all can exercise their free will to receive Christ's merits, and fulfil Christ's injunction to "be perfect as your Father in heaven is perfect" (Matthew 5:32).

Morgan's central message was that the Church was to be a religious institution consisting of Christians wholly dedicated to the observance of Christ's code of behaviour. Morgan insisted that God wanted his people to be holy and that he had given his people the means to accomplish perfection. A person's baptism has presented him with the unique opportunity to become a Christian, abandoning old pagan ways and leading a new life. We squander this opportunity when we lapse into old, comfortable habits of self-indulgence and careless pursuit of worldly things. Morgan's view of God's grace was broader than that of his opponents. He wrote, "This grace we do not allow to consist only in the law but also in the help of God . . . ."

Morgan believed that human beings began to sin from that moment when they became consciously able as children to imitate the sins of others, not because of some flawed nature forcing them to do so, but because they were ignorant of their true essence and potential. Their will had been corrupted by Adam's example of sin and the fallen world's habit of sin. To enable man to correct this flaw God first provided the Law. Although the Law failed, it allowed human beings to recognize the error of their ways and to become conscious of their sins. Mankind was still in possession of the capacity to live without sin, but was prevented by the inability to draw "upon the treasure of his soul"—the free will with which God had endowed him at creation.

The capacity to make choices and to translate them into right action is under a human's control and produces righteousness. But since Adam's sin and the Fall, our capacity to be righteous, despite being reinforced by the Law, has atrophied because of our failure to make the right use of this capacity to make choices. In order to restore our divinely endowed faculties, God has offered the opportunity of redemption by the saving death of Jesus Christ, who forgives our sins, restores our will, and sustains it by his own teaching and example.

Morgan wrote a commentary on St Paul's Letter to the Romans.[127] With reference to Paul's teaching in Romans 7:7–28, he points out that any enslavement to sin originates in a choice which becomes habitual through repetition. With reference to Romans 8:1–13 that people are weakened by the flesh, he points out that the flesh in itself is not sinful, it is the deeds of the flesh that are sinful. Not everyone is carnal: it is possible not to be carnal. This teaching is, I think, the *consensus fidelium* today. On the other hand, Paul's statement that "As in Adam all die, so in Christ shall all be made alive" is re-presented. He gives examples to show that there were a few righteous people even at the worst periods of Israel's sinning. It was nevertheless necessary for Christ to come and save humankind because humanity as a whole had lost touch with God. By coming as a second Adam, Christ showed us that it is possible to be in Adam and live a God-filled life. As Christ was in his manhood so we can be. His comment on Romans 8:25 is that God has foreknowledge of our free choices but that is different from fatalism.

Morgan's doctrine provides for a grace of creation, a grace of revelation, and a grace of redemption. It is God who, in the first place, has given man the possibility of doing good as his original endowment of grace and has confirmed and strengthened it by revelation and redemption through Jesus Christ.

It is an irony of history that at almost the same time as St Morgan of Wales was facing charges of heresy in Rome for having upbraided the wealthy and powerful of that city, St John Chrysostom was facing the same dilemma in the East. As Patriarch of Constantinople his primary concern was the misuse of wealth by the rich. In his reforms he made huge personal donations to the poor, cutting back on clerical pomp and extravagance. He was also outspoken in his condemnation of secular extravagance, and although beloved by many he made many influential enemies. Among those was the Eastern Empress Eudoxia (condemned by John for her vanity and lack of charity) and many prominent churchmen, including Theophilus of Alexandria (John's previously thwarted rival for the title of Patriarch of Constantinople). The Synod of Oak in 403, under the leadership of Theophilus, condemned John on twenty-nine charges, including an unsupported accusation of heresy and the charge of having personally attacked the Empress in a sermon. John was banished twice but continued his outspoken preaching. He died of exhaustion in Pontus. His body was returned to Constantinople thirty-one years later and was buried in the Church of the Apostles. Today, however, he is venerated as one of the Greek Doctors of the Church in the West and one of the Three Holy Hierarchs and Universal Teachers in the East, and a growing number of people believe that Pelagius is being similarly rehabilitated.

Pelagius's theology should be seen against the background of early fifth-century debates in Rome having to do with an anti-Manichean defence of the freedom of the will . . . and the character and transmission of original sin. It is in this context that we should see the Pelagian emphasis on the power to choose between good and evil as a God-given faculty of the soul, the right use of which is founded on the example of the Law and the teachings of Christ. His very high theology of creation led him also to deny original sin on the grounds that neither vice nor virtue is inborn. There is also a noticeable trend towards the communitarian values of the Christian vocation.

The story of Adam and Eve in a Garden of Eden is memorable. Over the years different wings of the Church put a construct on this story. The Orthodox Church describes Adam and Eve's "fall" as "O Happy Fault". The doctrines of human depravity and the inherently sinful nature of human flesh were taught by Gnostics, but early Christian apologists took great pains to counter them. They insisted God's future judgement of humanity implied humanity must have the ability to live righteously. However, Augustine used the term "original sin" to describe the innate sinfulness of all humans, a condition which is passed on by the sexual act of human reproduction. This idea was further developed as "total depravity" by certain Reformation teachers.[128]

Augustine has been regarded as the father of Western Christianity, both Roman and Reformed. Even the greatest fathers have blind spots or are children of their age. An increasing number of thinkers believe that a spirit of separation and schism crept into Christianity. Augustinians failed to stress that God in Trinity is eternally in every human being. We may deny or distance ourselves from God's presence in us, but ultimately "nothing can separate us from the love of God" (Romans 8:39).

In recent times, popular Christian voices have emerged who identify Pelagius with "Celtic Christianity" and with a positive view of nature and human nature. For example, David Cole writes:

> This idea that we, or the souls of every human being, are like a community living in peace, but that has been occupied by an invading army (what sin has done), means that the work of the cross is a driving out of the sin which occupies our inner being, restoring us back to what we were originally—living in peace with ourselves in good relationship with our Maker. With this understanding the work of the cross, the driving out of the sin in us, could perhaps be seen as the never-ending work of becoming more like Christ, and is 'the releasing of what we essentially are'—perfect in righteousness—a perfect reflection of the divine image. As Pelagius himself suggests in his *Letter to Demetrias*, each individual is capable of living a holy and righteous life:

> Before the arrival of our Lord and Saviour some are reported
> to have lived holy and righteous lives; how much more possible
> must we believe that to be after the light of his coming, now that
> we have been instructed by the grace of Christ and reborn as
> better men: purified and cleansed by his blood, encouraged by
> his example to pursue perfect righteousness.[129] [130]

The world faces an epidemic of gun, knife and hate crimes. Jordan Peterson, the Canadian Professor of Psychology and author of the best-selling *Twelve Rules for Life*, argues that most of this is caused by young men who can't find status. They feel trapped in a culture where hope of advancement or worth is extinguished.

In his book *Listening to the heartbeat of God: A Celtic Spirituality*, Philip Newell suggests that "for Pelagius, evil was rather like an occupying army. The people yearn for liberation, but are bound by the forces of evil. Redemption, therefore, can be understood in terms of a setting free, a releasing of what we essentially are."[131]

Pelagius offers us infinite worth because God is in the core of our being; he offers us the power of possibility. He refuses to extinguish the possibility that, in Christ, we can live on earth as it is in heaven:

> Whenever I have to speak on the subject of moral instruction and
> the conduct of a holy life, it is my practice first to demonstrate the
> power and quality of human nature and to show what it is capable
> of achieving, and then go on to encourage the mind of the listener
> to consider the idea of different kinds of virtues, in case it may be
> of little or no profit to him to be summoned to pursue ends which
> he has perhaps assumed hitherto to be beyond his reach; for we
> can never enter onto the path of virtue unless we have hope as
> our guide and companion and if every effort expended in seeking
> something is nullified in effect by despair of ever finding it . . .

The 2017 edition of the Iona Community's *Iona Abbey Worship Book* contains these words that reflect Pelagius: "We affirm God's goodness at the heart of humanity, planted more deeply than all that is wrong."

CHAPTER 9

The world awaits a re-awakening that cleanses, earths and re-connects

In 1999, Ian Bradley wrote *Celtic Christianity: Making Myths and Chasing Dreams*. In this he charts the course and describes the main characteristics of six waves of Celtic Christian revivalism and chronicles the "love-affair" that many have had with Celtic Christianity, in which "myth-making, legend-building, inventing and reinventing history for propagandist purposes have all played a significant role".[132]

I think this description has truth, but it is only half the truth. The limitation of Bradley's approach is that it treats these diverse revivals, each with widely different motivations, as if they are one brushstroke. Jesus's words "By their fruits you shall know them" might be a better test for each expression.

He regards the fifth to seventh centuries as the foundation period, sometimes known as the Age of the Saints, to which subsequent revivals look back. Only a few *Lives* of Celtic saints survive from this period (no doubt many were lost in Viking raids) and these were all written on the continent of Europe, for example the *Lives* of Samson, Columbanus and Fursey. He suggests that "the first and perhaps most influential rediscovery and reinvention" was the writing in Ireland or Britain of some one hundred hagiographies in Latin, covering sixty saints, more than a hundred years after they had died. The need for these was perhaps prompted by the Great Plague of 665, and a slippage in standards in some monasteries whose monks lost their first ardour. The cult of Brigid is a pre-eminent example. This put spiritual enthusiasm above historical accuracy.

Rationalist twentieth-century Christians who de-mythologized the Gospels made mincemeat of these hagiographies, whereas charismatic Christians who rediscovered the operations of the Spirit in a postmodern world relished them. Currently, many Christians see no necessary conflict between Reason and Spirit. A hagiography is not a biography: it explores a saint from the viewpoint of what God worked in them.

Bradley's second wave of Celtic revival relates to attempts by Welsh and Irish to resist cultural absorption by their Anglo-Norman colonizers between 1070 and 1220, and to attempts by the colonizers to make their centralizing rule acceptable. Before that, the new Anglo-Saxon rulers of Cornwall astutely encouraged the cult of Celtic saints. St Germans was made the seat of an independent Cornish diocese in 994 and all but one of the Cornish religious houses listed in the 1086 Domesday Book were Celtic foundations. With the coming of the Anglo-Normans, episcopal uniformity in dioceses and Benedictine uniformity in monasteries replaced the local character typical of Celtic Christian communities. However, they often appropriated Celtic foundations and figureheads to legitimize their new regime. William the Conqueror made a pilgrimage to St David's; all this was part of a wider revival of interest in saints throughout Western Christendom.

Sometimes the power of authentic Celtic spirituality broke through the political dynamics. Bradley reminds us of Aldwin, an English monk who was Prior of Winchcombe Abbey. Prompted by reading Bede's accounts of Northumbrian monasteries, he set off in 1070 with two companions to seek a life of poverty and solitude in the land of Aidan and Cuthbert. Though they found only ruins, at Jarrow they covered some outbuildings in thatch and wood and lived there for several years. Scotland's devout Catholic Queen Margaret is often portrayed as nothing but a Romanizer. Yet she actively endowed "certain monasteries of the Irish tradition", including a community on St Serf's Island and some monks who remained in the Columba tradition on Iona.[133]

Ian Bradley constructs a third Celtic revival that lasts for 600 years from 1250 to 1850! This is nationalistic and denominationalistic. Small countries vied for legitimacy or precedence by claiming Celtic saints as their patrons. Roman Catholic and Reformation churches vied to claim that they were the true heirs to the original Celtic Christianity. An example of this is the biography of David by Bishop Rhygyfarch, who wanted his diocese to have primacy at a time when Anselm, Archbishop of Canterbury, wanted to subsume it. By portraying David as an archbishop, he hoped to prevent this. His *Life* has been described as "the last defensive cry of the Celtic church before it was swallowed up by the Normans".[134] Yet genuine love of the holiness of their local saints survived the politics. One can detect this in a *Life of Illtud* written about 1140 by a monk at Llantwit Major and incorporated into a book of the lives of several Welsh saints compiled about 1200. Here, the attraction of holiness trumps any desire to advance the claims of the place.

Although Cuthbert remained popular among the people, the massive development of the cult of Cuthbert by the Benedictine authorities at Durham was dictated by territorial ambitions. There is a danger that Durham's current use of Cuthbert to make it a centre of pilgrimage has similar motives. In various lands a whole range of Celtic saints were drafted in to promote the ambitions of political and ecclesiastical causes. Saints' *Lives*, festivals and church dedications were promoted according to the secular heroes of the time.

In Scotland, monarchs made claims that they were heirs of Celtic heritage in order to ward off English claims of dominance. Seven out of ten Scottish dioceses are centred on old Celtic monastic sites. In Ireland, both its overlords and its new Roman Catholic orders appropriated Celtic foundations. *Lives* of saints were commissioned by the powers that be that aggrandized the simplicity of the original stories—this was true of *Lives* of *Ninian, Columba, Patrick, Kentigern* and many others. The notion of the epic journey, such as that of Brendan, captured popular imagination. The legend of the Holy Grail, a development of the Arthurian mythic cult, captured the imagination of English and French knights.

Cistercians promoted many Celtic saints. A Cistercian monk incorporated Celtic Christianity into the newly formulated Roman Catholic doctrine of purgatory through his fictional book *St. Patrick's Purgatory*. This period offers many examples of making God in our own image. Personal penance was replaced by public proclamation. On the other hand, the notion of a pure, ancient Celtic Britain chimed with Protestant patriotism. Celtic crosses and church dedications were restored.

There were, indeed, romanticists. Perhaps inspired by Robert Burns in Scotland, in Wales Edward Williams (1747–1826), more commonly known by his bardic name, Iolo Morganwg, rewrote the history of Welsh literature and letters. He collected or invented folk songs and the fiction of an aboriginal Welsh literature.

The humble, incarnational spirit of the best of the Celtic founders was lost under an avalanche of claims and counterclaims. But it was not extinguished: some believe that the Franciscan and other mendicant orders were inspired by the Celtic *peregrini*.

The nationalistic form that the Celtic revival of 1250–1850 took is still a danger. I meet USA Christians who are drawn to Celtic spiritual movements because they define themselves against the English. Some of them study Scottish revivals and their passion is to pray for revival along the old Celtic lines in Scotland today—but they make Scotland as much their god as God himself. The fact that Putin's Russia has revived on the back of the Russian Orthodox Church, into which huge sums from the state have been poured, warns us of this ever-present danger.

Bradley's list of Celtic revivals seems rather ad hoc. He ignores the Celtic movements in the Great Dispersion from Celtic to New World countries during the nineteenth century. During the Irish potato famine from 1845–52, one million died and up to two million emigrated to countries such as Canada, the USA and Australia. By 1850, the USA had three million Irish residents and three million from other Celtic lands, as well as more than this from England. The Scottish enclosures—the forced eviction of tenants by landowners—and general economic depression caused mass migration from Scotland. In the first half of the nineteenth century, 59 per cent of Canadian settlers from the UK were Scots-born. From 1853, however, 50 per cent of emigrating Scots chose to settle in the USA, and by 1850 Scots made up a quarter of the population in New Zealand.

The Kernow (Cornish National) movement is strong in Australia. In 1859, large amounts of copper were discovered in South Australia. Many hundreds of Cornish miners moved there with their families, and introduced things like Cornish wrestling, pasties, Methodism and brass bands. So many Cornish people settled in this area that it became known as "Australia's Little Cornwall". The Kernewek Lowender Copper Coast

Cornish Festival is held in the coastal towns of Wallaroo, Moonta and Kadina and welcomes approximately 45,000 people to celebrate the area's Cornish heritage. In Nova Scotia, Celtic festivals and networks thrive. The St Patrick's Day Parade in New York attracts around two million spectators. Many of the Celtic festivals in the USA and Canada replicate aspects of Scotland's Highland Games or celebrate Celtic folk music. The Irish Global Diaspora Directory lists 360 organizations in the USA, Canada and Australasia that keep some aspect of Irish heritage alive. I would summarize this ongoing revival as folk heritage. There is nothing much wrong with it, but it is not Christianity, though for some it inter-links music, cultural and spiritual strands that are missing from the less holistic cultures in which they live.

The Celtic Revival in English Literature by Humphrey Milford (Oxford University Press) is one of many publications that describe a revival of poetry focused on the national identities of England, Ireland, Scotland and Wales that had become grey among the mass production of industrialization. This movement is known as the Romantic or Celtic Twilight movement. Its foremost poets included Wordsworth, Shelley, Southey and Byron.

This was part of a wider renewal in the nineteenth and twentieth centuries of aspects of Celtic culture—both pagan and Christian. Artists and writers drew on the traditions of Gaelic literature, Welsh-language literature and "Celtic art". William Sharp (d. 1905), the Scottish poet who also wrote under the pseudonym of Fiona McLeod, met with W. B. Yeats in some kind of Celtic bardic group which was in part neo-Druid. Such poets, along with others such as Edward Plunkett and Lady Gregory, were part of what was known as the Celtic Revival. This multi-faceted revival covered many countries in Europe, but its most memorable incarnation is probably the Irish Literary Revival, which helped to ignite Irish nationalism.

In many, but not all, facets the revival came to represent a reaction to mechanization. This is particularly true in Ireland, where the relationship between the archaic and the modern was antagonistic, where history was fractured, and where, according to Terry Eagleton, "as a whole [the nation] had not leapt at a bound from tradition to modernity".[135] At times this romantic view of the past resulted in historically inaccurate portrayals, such as the promotion of noble savage stereotypes of the Irish people and Scottish Highlanders, as well as a racialized view that referred to the Irish, whether positively or negatively, as a separate race.

The Welsh antiquarian and author Iolo Morganwg fed the growing fascination in all things Brittonic by founding the Gorsedd, which (along with his writings) would in turn spark the Neo-Druidism movement.

Interest in Scottish Gaelic culture greatly increased during the onset of the Romantic period in the late eighteenth century, with James Macpherson's *Ossian* achieving international fame, along with the novels of Sir Walter Scott and the poetry and song lyrics of the London-based Irishman Thomas Moore, Byron's friend and executor. Even Beethoven was commissioned to produce a set of arrangements of Scottish folk songs. As elsewhere, in what was then the United Kingdom of the whole archipelago, this encouraged and fed off a rise in nationalism, which was especially intense in Ireland. It embraced a romantic revival of neo-pagan Druidry, and new archaeological work on ancient sites in Celtic lands. In art, Celtic motifs began to be used in varied contexts.

The Celtic Revival was an international movement that was also reflected in designs of new buildings, Art Nouveau, metalwork and even tattoos. As late as the 1960s this movement was reflected in the media, fiction and films.

Should all that is associated with these Celtic revivals be dismissed as solely romantic and fictional, and no longer relevant to modern life? Perhaps much of it should, but I think not all. Meg Llewellyn writes:

> For both Christians and Pagans, the long-ago Celts seem to offer an alternative way of looking at life, a more holistic way that perceives the sacred in the ordinary, that spiritually communes with Nature, and that consciously seeks to bless both the human and the natural worlds. We yearn for what the Celts had, and many of us seek to recreate it in our own lives.[136]

Lady Augusta Gregory (1852–1932) was an Irish writer and playwright who, by her translations of Irish legends, her peasant comedies and fantasies based on folklore, and her work for the Abbey Theatre, played a considerable part in the late nineteenth-century Irish literary renascence.

Susan Power Bratton unearths the criteria by which Lady Gregory selected material.[137] She shaped ancient materials around her constructs. She was a convinced Christian. She worked closely with W. B. Yeats, who wrote that those "who would re-awaken imaginative tradition by making old songs live again or by gathering stories into books" are taking part in the gospel, the telling of the good news that God lives among us and we are called to make divine justice, generosity and gentleness real in the world around us.

Allied to these is a revival of Celtic languages in Cornwall, Ireland, Scotland and Wales. Galicia, in Spain, also enjoyed a Celtic revival, especially in music, following the repression of its culture under the Franco regime. How much this is a pure celebration of unique identity, and how much an anti-English, anti-globalist reaction, is up for debate. There seems little grounding in the Christ-like values of hospitality that marks the monastic expressions of Celtic Christianity. A criticism levelled at the current Celtic spirituality springtime is that it draws from modern ideas and is not therefore historically valid. Such modern ideas might include the equality of men and women, ecology, human developmental processes, the search for roots, the concept of flow in areas such as art and music.

The Celtic revival that began in the 1980s and 1990s was specifically Christian. As I mentioned in chapter one, it is sometimes claimed that this began among Protestant evangelical charismatics, such as Michael Mitton, Director of Anglican Renewal Ministries, who yearned for "something more". But before that David Adam became a best-selling author of Celtic prayers and meditations. He was a coal miner, an Anglo-Catholic and a mystic. Roman Catholics were also part of this revival. An American Benedictine, Timothy Joyce, wrote *Celtic Christianity: A Sacred Tradition, a Vision of Hope*, and an Irish Carmelite, Noel O'Donoghue, wrote many books and taught at Edinburgh University about Celtic spirituality. Many Orthodox have recognized a kinship between Celtic and Orthodox spirituality. I welcomed to Lindisfarne two students sponsored by the Russian Patriarch to study the links between Orthodox and Celtic art and spirituality.

What of the future? Recently, I launched daily emails on alternate weeks on "The Way". These seek to lay spiritual foundations that will take us through the twenty-first century into a space age.[138] In one of these I quote from a talk the Archbishop of Canterbury gave to ecumenical new monastics at Lambeth Palace on 28 March 2014:

> Alasdair MacIntyre in *After Virtue*, as I am sure most of you know, speaks of a new dark age on the last page of that very interesting book, and talks of the need for a new, and, as he puts it, doubtless very different St Benedict. Perhaps that will not be a person but a movement, groups of people, even, because again, in almost all cases religious renewal starts with groups in prayer, not merely a single charismatic hero figure, although those are often the ones we remember and canonise. We are not looking for a Nietzschean superman, but a collection of fragile disciples who know that they have a tendency to betray and abandon Jesus and who gather in obedience so that they may receive the Paraclete.
>
> What might that look like? I have no idea; it is, after all, in the mind of God. But today's gathering . . . is to suggest that we need a wild burst of fresh and Spirit-fuelled imagination about religion in the twenty-first century. It will be embedded in its traditions, but as in all past renewals of religion it will also be different. Above all it will be spontaneous, not top down and under control. . . . What institutional changes are needed? How do the churches (we are not all Anglicans here) obstruct you, hinder you when we should celebrate and support? What re-imagination do we need?

When people feel that "things fall apart, the centre cannot hold" (Yeats) it is understandable that they want to create some protected "zones of stability". But if God is in the falling apart, might he not want leaders to abandon themselves to the process, and use tools that help them to navigate the ocean of flux without hitting the reefs? The Irish "pilgrims for the love of God" who travelled across the Continent did more to re-evangelize Dark Age Europe than the top down missions or stay-put monasteries. Aidan and the Irish monks model a way of living amid "the changes and chances" of this fleeting life. Communities who live this spirit today are not end points but launching pads.

In the nineteenth century, John Henry Newman wrote *The Development of Doctrine* in relation to the Christian religion as a whole. He likened the original deposit of the Christian faith to seeds. He traced many later developments in the Church. He concluded that developments that can be compared to the maturing and flowering of the original seeds were valid and necessary, only growths that were alien to the seeds were to be rejected. That principle can, I suggest, be appropriately applied to each development within Christianity, including the Celtic.

"Ignatian spirituality" today differs from the spirituality of Ignatius Loyola, the founder of the Jesuits, from whom it takes its name. For example, a typical Ignatian retreat will draw on psychological insights of C. G. Jung. Ignatius had never heard of Myers Briggs personality types, and his view of the Devil probably differs from the views of many current Ignatian retreat leaders. Ignatius did, however, encourage the practice of meditating upon a passage of Scripture, using the imagination, asking certain questions, and making a response to God. These practices are retained, although other elements have changed. There have been developments.

Benedictine spirituality has been greatly adapted and developed through the ages. The Rule of St Benedict was drawn up for a group of lay monks who lived in one house in Italy in the sixth century. Yet today light is sought from it for a multitude of contexts which Benedict could not have dreamed of. I have before me a leaflet produced by The Leadership Institute. The compiler, Rob Mackintosh, comes up with "nine disciplines of leadership", which, to his mind, can be ferreted out of Benedict's Rule. He admits, however, that "in each generation the Rule has been reinterpreted in the light of current needs and social context. Few monastic communities would now hand to the abbot or prior the degree of power and authority expressed in the Rule. Questions of discipline, of authority and obedience have needed constant reappraisal through a search for enduring principles behind the text of the Rule."[139]

Why should this process of development be any different in relation to Celtic spirituality? It is true that Ignatian and Benedictine spirituality each primarily look back to one founder and one document, the Spiritual Exercises and the Rule. Celtic Christian spirituality is more analogous to the New Testament documents, which were sifted for centuries before the Church drew up its canon of twenty-seven authorized writings, which reflect the lives and teaching of the founder and twelve apostles. Celtic Christianity has its key documents (St Patrick's Declaration, Columbanus's writings, Adomnan's *Life of Columba*, Bede's *History* for example) and its roll call of leading saints in each land (for example, Patrick, Brigid, Brendan and Kevin stand out in Ireland; Samson, Illtyd, David and Petroc stand out in Wales and western Britain; Aidan, Hilda, Oswald and Cuthbert stand out in England). Authenticity in the handling of the early material and of the process of reappraisal is what marks out the worthwhile from the sham.

Religious and political movements feed on myths of a golden age. These have a place, for where there is no vision, societies tend to spiral downwards. But history is evidence that merely Utopian movements do not last. An obvious example from the last century is Marxist Communism: the Utopian ideal of a classless society foundered upon the rock of human nature. One reason why Christianity has survived huge vicissitudes and lasted for 2,000 years is that its founder earthed it in a cowshed, a cross, a corpus of teachings and a community. But during the last millennium churches divorced the cowshed from the spires, the cross from the circle of life, the teaching corpus from a "my idea is right" mindset, and community from market-brand churches. In a post-truth culture, everyone and every church "does what is right in his own eyes". Few are the followers of the Way of Reality.

Ian Bradley, referring to his Celtic Christianity: Making Myths and Chasing Dreams, states that he is happy to "dedicate this more sober, and, I trust, scholarly volume to those who dream dreams and see visions" and concludes: "If Celtic Christianity, however reconstructed and reshaped, can help us not just to dream but to put our dreams into reality by changing ourselves and our world and moving forward in imitation of Christ and towards the Kingdom of God, then that for me is its ultimate justification."[140]

The Christian Church is "built upon the foundation of the apostles and prophets, Jesus Christ himself as the chief cornerstone" (Ephesians 2:14). The twelve apostles were Jews, but churches in non-Jewish cultures do not say "they are not our apostles". Celtic Christianity is built upon its apostles and prophets, Jesus Christ himself as the chief cornerstone.

These apostles, too, are universal and archetypal: believers from cultures far from Celtic-speaking countries may still embrace them as their own.

The Celtic Christian tradition at its best corrects this imbalance, cleanses the edifices of the false ego, and earths Christianity.

There is something more yet. We may discern in some unfolding societies, not a Celtic revival, but a fresh birthing. Water from both indigenous and Celtic well-springs flows into the emerging society and transforms it. David Tacey points out that the power of the land and the influence of aboriginal culture are activating primordial levels of the Euro-Australian psyche, stirring its deeper layers.[141] Tacey believes that a version of ancient Celtic spirituality is being awakened and stirred to new life in Australia. One can see many signs of this in Australian folk culture, where the attempt to "grow down" into Australian soil has the effect of revitalizing Celtic roots, giving rise to a redeeming of primal roots through Christ.[142]

Those who draw water from these well-springs become part of a back-to-the-future movement. Ever-replenished renewal comes from the ever-living water. They share in the birth of a new society.

In his last book, *Brief Answers to the Big Questions*, Stephen Hawking concluded that we live in a universe governed by rational laws, and that "one could define God as the embodiment of the laws of nature".[143] We are now entering a new phase of human history. He thinks that either a nuclear confrontation or environmental catastrophe will cripple the earth at some point in the next thousand years. He hopes we will find a way to relocate homo sapiens on some other planet. There is no time to wait for Darwinian evolution to make us more intelligent and better natured. Nationalisms increase. We are a selfish species. We have mapped DNA, which means we can read "the book of life", so we can start writing in corrections. The task of Celtic spirituality is to offer the world a way of "writing in corrections" which is freed from nationalistic and denominationalistic constructs.

CHAPTER 10

Restorative justice and spiritual fitness are society's lungs

"Thou hast conquered, O pale Galilean; the world has grown grey from thy breath." In these words, A. C. Swinburne's poem "Hymn to Proserpine" laments the rise of Christianity for displacing the delights associated with this pagan goddess. This kind of criticism, which Swinburne levelled at Christianity as a whole, has found a special target in the many ascetics who spread from Egyptian deserts to Celtic lands and adopted strict penitential disciplines.

Ian Bradley writes in his article in *The Tablet* of 23 June 2018:

> Key texts such as St. Patrick's Confession, the prayers attributed to Columba, the sermons of his contemporary and namesake Columbanus, and the lives of the early Welsh saints all express a deeply conservative and orthodox faith, centered on human sin and the Fall, a deep antipathy to the things of this world and a strong emphasis on constant penitence and contrition . . . . The largest single category of original manuscript sources that have survived from the golden age of Celtic monasticism are the Irish Penitentials—long lists of precise punishments prescribed for every conceivable lapse from the superhuman standard of behaviour expected of those living under monastic discipline. Like the surviving monastic rules, they enjoin severe regimes of self-mortification, bordering on the masochistic.

The Oxford Dictionary defines masochistic as deriving (especially sexual) gratification from one's own pain or humiliation. I find little evidence from the texts that this was what these penances were about. The purpose of penance was to produce fruits. Hospitality, a universal Christian virtue in which the Celts excelled, was a fruit of denial—the opposite of selfishness.

Katherine Lack draws a contrasting conclusion to that of Ian Bradley: "When set down baldly, in black and white, (the Rule of Columbanus) does not necessarily seem an attractive way of life." However, despite the austere and ascetic manner of the Rule "to the Franks it was heroic Christianity; it related directly to what they heard from the Bible, in a way that the existing continental church, so often urban, established and rich, did not".[144]

Probably all contemporary readers would condemn the practice of whipping someone who coughed during the divine liturgy. However, we might wish not to lose the point of this. I shared the daily liturgy at St Mary's, Lindisfarne, with its then vicar, David Adam. He would employ strategies and go to great lengths to avoid coughing except during an "Amen". It was a conscious discipline. He doubtless thought that he paid a small price for preserving the unity and focus of the corporate liturgy—the beauty of harmony: nothing but the best for God.

Some contemporary Christians disagree with the penitential approach, even if it is not alleged to be masochistic, because they think Christianity should be life-affirming rather than life-denying. But can these be two sides of the same coin? Life-affirming Christians are generally enthusiastic about pilgrimage, yet pilgrimage means setting aside what we want in order to accept what life brings and to accept the people God brings alongside us. This is a form of denial of our false ego. Finnian, who attracted the great monastic leaders to his famed monastery at Clonard, used to sleep on a stone bed with a chain around him. There is no hint that these others copied that practice, or that Finnian required others to copy this custom, but they were inspired by his life of selfless devotion to live for Christ alone. Many people who despise the crude methods of penance would assess them differently if they understood the joy of spiritual fitness.

Much penance in Ireland was akin to a criminal justice programme in a modern state. Those who had injured their neighbour needed to make recompense. In our criminal justice systems some pay a fine, others go to prison, where they have to go without comforts, and others do community service. Modern critics of early Celtic monasticism sometimes fail to distinguish between penalties for crimes which the local ruler imposed on lawbreakers through the tribal monastery, which took on a role played by modern police forces, and disciplines monastic ascetics volunteered for. The quite large collection of Irish Handbooks of Penance suggests that customs varied widely in different places. In some places the monasteries combined their spiritual role with that of local law-keeper.[145] They issued commutations for a host of offences and one form of penalty could be substituted for another. For example, a fine could be paid instead of confiscation of property. If a priest killed a neighbour, he must be exiled for seven years. A thief must either go to prison or go on pilgrimage until he has restored double what he has stolen. Canings are mentioned in at least one of the penitentials. Fasts were required for some offences, but one equivalent was to spend three days with a dead saint in a tomb without food or sleep, chanting psalms! Another penance was to sing all 150 psalms with the arms stretched out in the shape of the cross. Gildas, whose British penitential was copied in Ireland, prescribed abstinence from meat and wine for one year for certain offences. No Christian institution would impose such penances today, but the principles behind them are not obsolete.

Kenney describes these penances as a "fixed tariff".[146] This suggests a rigid system of penalties for offences committed. But Ludwig Bieler, in tune with more recent work by writers such as Thomas O'Loughlin and Hugh Connolly, maintains that the Irish penitentials take pains to make the "penance appropriate to attitude rather than acts". Bieler quotes a passage from the Penitential of Finnian, usually accepted as the earliest complete example of the penitential genre and dating from about 525–550, to back up his argument:

> If a cleric is wrathful or envious or backbiting, gloomy or greedy ... there is this penance for them, until they are plucked forth and eradicated from our hearts: . . . we shall continue in weeping and tears day and night so long as these things are turned over in our heart. But by contraries, as we said, let us make haste to cure contraries and to cleanse away the faults from our hearts and introduce virtues in their places. Patience must arise for

wrathfulness; kindliness, the love of God and of one's neighbour, for envy; for detraction, restraint of the heart and tongue; for dejection, spiritual joy; for greed, liberality.[147]

Ascetics who migrated to Egypt's deserts to follow sacred disciplines inspired wealthy believers in cities such as Rome. Villas and palaces of many great third-century Roman families were dedicated to monastic purposes. One of these was Marcella's palace on the Aventine, one of Rome's seven hills. What they heard from the visiting Athanasius about Antony and the lives of the Egyptian solitaries, and about Pachomius's monasteries and the rules he had given to monks and nuns, excited in Marcella's family and friends a desire to imitate these ascetics in their own setting. Her ten-year-old daughter Asella built a cell in the palace and practised being a nun. Her time was taken up with prayer and contemplation, and needlework for the poor. Upon being widowed, Marcella turned her house into a cloister, wore coarse clothes and sold her jewellery for the benefit of the poor. Many other women led similar lives and placed themselves under her guidance.[148]

The nobility in Ireland, though they lacked the grandeur of Rome's palaces, were also soon aflame with the desire to emulate the Egyptian ascetics. Brigid, Darerca and Ita were but three of many women from ruling families who adopted a rule and became Brides of Christ. The eighth-century *Catalogue of the Saints of Ireland* refers to a Third Order of Anchorites who settled in cells in uninhabited places, lived on herbs, water and the gifts of the people, wore a variety of tonsures and observed diverse rules and liturgies.[149]

Several texts communicated ascetic monastic ideals to the far west of Europe: Athanasius's *Life of Antony*, Sulpicius Severus's *Life of St Martin of Tours*, Cassian's *Conferences and Institutes*, and the influence of Honorius, who trained many, perhaps including Patrick, at his pioneering island monastery of Lerins. Professor E. G. Bowen of the University College of Wales, Aberystwyth, believed that the whole of south-western Britain was subject to the influence of the Egyptian Church in the fifth and sixth centuries: John Cassian first expounded the idea that sin is more a medical than a legal matter. Penance was a cure for sickness more than a punishment for sins. Sin requires diagnoses and appropriate, restorative remedies.

The persecution of Christians in the Roman provinces of Egypt and the Near East caused many there to flee to the desert. At first, they lived solitary lives practising extremes of hardship. Later, however, some came together in large or small groups for work and worship, and so renounced the world. They were visited in the desert from time to time by leading Christians in the West and these, on returning home, set up their own monasteries in imitation of those of the desert. Lerins, near Marseilles, Ligugé, and Marmoutier, near Tours, are cases in point. The pattern of these Gaulish monasteries ultimately spread to Britain. Modern archaeologists have been able to show that the lands around the eastern Mediterranean, including Egypt, Palestine, Asia Minor and the Aegean islands, were in post-Roman times in direct trade contact with south-western Britain. Certain types of wheel-made pottery, clearly non-British in character, have been found in recent years in southern Ireland, Wales and south-west England, often stamped with Christian symbols. Along these western sea routes, full monastic life, perhaps starting at Tintagel on the north coast of Cornwall between 470 and 500, arrived. The monastic pattern spread rapidly afterwards to such sites as Llanilltyd Fawr, Nantcarban, Llandaff, Caldey, Glastonbury, St David's, Llanbadarn Fawr and other places in Wales before passing over to central and southern Ireland.[150]

It is indisputable that the teachings and practices of the Eastern monks reached Ireland and played an important part in the development of this island. This is explored in *The Mediterranean Legacy in Early Celtic Christianity: A Journey from Armenia to Ireland*.[151] Ireland in the sixth century has been described as "the outer ripple of the great monastic movement of the Greek and Coptic churches of the East".

St Martin's diocese at Tours became perhaps the most influential in Gaul: its hub was the hermits' cells in the caves and fields beside the River Loire where Martin himself also dwelt. Cells and small monastic communities inspired by Martin spread throughout Britain and Ireland. They were often called "White Houses". St Brigid co-governed her double monasteries of women and men with a bishop who was a hermit. The great faith communities at Glendalough and Aran in Ireland grew up around hermits who attracted people to holy living. Cronan, who spent his teens in Connaught, founded as many as fifty settlements for hermits. As soon as he found a suitable spot, he would gather young would-be hermits, school them in the sacred truths and practices, give them charge of the community and move on to another place. He founded a large hermitage in a bog at Monaincha, but when a group of pilgrims got lost and had to spend a night in a nearby bog, he relocated to Roscrea, near the ancient road from Dublin to Limerick.

It is recorded that Samson and David both retreated from Llantwit Major to Caldey Island, and that Dyfrig made his Lenten retreat on Bardsey, where he also returned to die. David's own original community, to judge from Rhygyfarch's *Life of David*, may well also have been of this kind. A further type of monastic lifestyle is visible, however, in Samson's rejection of Caldey and his retreat to a cave where, together with a small number of other hermits, he pursued a more uncompromising vocation.[152]

Even leaders of large and busy faith communities such as Columba would keep the vigils and go away to live as hermits for days or weeks or years. This tradition was transplanted into the early English Church. Cuthbert was nine years a hermit on the Inner Farne Isle before he was persuaded to become a missionary bishop for two years before returning to his cell to die. Chad, one of the first boys at Aidan's school at Lindisfarne, founded the large Midlands diocese. He made its hub a group of hermits' cells where he himself lived.

This tradition also continued long in Wales. Gerald of Wales noted in his late twelfth-century *Description of Wales*: "Nowhere can you see hermits and anchorites who are more ascetical and spiritually committed than in Wales."

What were their disciplines? It is true that the only sixth-century written monastic rule is that of Columbanus, which was written for solitary "soldiers of Christ" in front-line overseas mission and is not suited to settled conditions in a modern plural society. That does not mean there is nothing to learn from it. Columbanus's monastic communities in Europe had drawing power. The brothers were real and contrasted with the artificial protocols attached to the Frankish aristocrats who became bishops of dioceses. Such was their drawing power that aristocratic Frankish women started monasteries with a similar ethos for women.

Those in other walks of life may learn from Columbanus's advice to solitaries. This rule is influenced by Basil the Great and Cassian, and it probably reflects the ascetical earlier Rule of Comgall, the founder of the Irish monastery at Bangor, where Columbanus trained. Columbanus also supplied detailed rules for the wellbeing of the monastic household and for correction of faults. These rules, and the penitentials associated with them, the first written by Gildas of Britain, emphasize healing the eight major sins by developing their opposite virtues, constant Scripture meditation, and frequent, transparent sharing with a soul friend.

The following is a paraphrase of items in Columbanus's Rule:

> Let our bearing towards one another be that of Christ, honouring and listening intently, in particular to those in oversight who focus the unity of the community. Never grumble or hit back.
>
> Only speak when God gives you something to say. Avoid mindless or boastful talk.
>
> Eat and drink nothing that overloads the stomach or confuses the mind.
>
> Possess only what you need or what you can offer as love gifts.
>
> Live simply in order to purge vices and foster perpetual love of God.
>
> Cultivate humility and purity.

Columbanus's Rule concludes:

> Follow the rhythm of the seasons in corporate worship; pray together for longer during the long summer days.
>
> In your private prayer and study go with the ebb and flow: Pay heed to the season of your life, to your temperament, ability, and energy levels. The ceaseless prayer of the heart, not external uniformity, is what binds everyone together.
>
> Develop wisdom, balance, discernment of good and evil, excess and moderation, growth into wholeness, knowing what justice requires, the fruits of the Spirit and humility.

Take time to often seek counsel from a wise senior person.
Do not make decisions on your own that should first have been
considered with your soul friend. Beware of proud independence.
Watch that you do not avoid taking counsel because you secretly
nourish your own desires.

Accept the discipline of one spiritual father; love and trust him
with everything. In fellowship with all the brothers learn this virtue
from one and that virtue from another. Never judge another.

It seems likely that the earliest forms of penance were not penalties for
crimes, they were voluntary spiritual fitness programmes. They developed
in the deserts, where Christ's followers volunteered to replace the eight
vices with the eight virtues through demanding spiritual practices. In 375,
Evagrius developed a list of eight evil thoughts (*logismoi*), or temptations,
from which all sinful behaviour springs. This list was intended to serve
a diagnostic purpose: to help readers identify the process of temptation,
their own strengths and weaknesses, and the remedies available for
overcoming temptation. Evagrius stated: "The first thought of all is that
of love of self"; after this the eight patterns of evil thought are gluttony,
greed, sloth, sorrow, lust, anger, vainglory and pride.[153]

The Christians who undertook these penances were wholehearted
volunteers. They were like those who offer to undertake the extreme
rigours of commando troops in a great cause for the common good. They
volunteered because they were in love with God, not because they were
masochists. The principle behind them is the stripping of our false ego
until nothing but God's love is left.

It seems this emphasis on penance spread to Britain and from the
British Church to Ireland.[154] *The Cambrai Homily*, the oldest written
text in Irish, sees discipleship in terms of Jesus's injunction to "take up
your cross and follow me". It explores two ways of doing this, fasting and
penance. Fasting is not from something evil so much as for something,
for the good of our neighbour.

In her online essay on Celtic Christianity, Janet Tanner argues that

these handbooks for dealing with the sinfulness of ordained,
monastic and lay men and women not only emerged suddenly, but

in some cases were in common use across the whole of Christian Europe and into the Latin heartlands within a few generations. They became the basis for building a whole theological edifice around forgiveness, responding to the undeniable fact of the ongoing sinfulness of baptized Christians. This marked a profound change in theology. Christianity became more of a journey into holiness than a once-and-for-all conversion—as O'Loughlin puts it, 'the life-long struggle to grow more like Christ'.[155]

Hugh Connolly makes a case for the contemporary relevance and significance of the ancient Irish handbooks of penance.[156] After placing the penitentials in their cultural and historical context, he undertakes a lengthy textual analysis of the works from the point of view of one of their central organizing principles—the eight capital sins that were inherited from John Cassian. In the final chapter, Connolly explores the symbolism of the penitentials—the judicial model, the medical model of disease and healing, and the pilgrimage model. The penitentials appeared in Western Europe when the harsh system of non-repeatable public penance was waning, to be replaced with repeatable, private penance or confession.

The Rule of Columba, a copy of which survives in the Burgundian Library, Brussels, is thought by scholars to have been composed in the eighth or ninth century by an anonymous scribe. It is written for anchorites, or solitaries, who lived alone, but within reach of other solitaries, and who related to the Columban family of communities. It is reasonable to presume that the author thought he was writing in the spirit of the Columban tradition. This paraphrase gives a flavour of the ideals in this document:

> If your conscience leads you to keep away from crowds, be alone in a separate place near a major city.
>
> Always have a naked spirit in imitation of Christ and the Evangelists.
>
> Put whatever little possessions you have at the disposal of your senior (soul friend).
>
> Make sure your dwelling is enclosed and has one door.

Invite several members of your nearest monastery to study the Bible with you on Christian festivals.

Refuse entry to those who want to gossip or talk about trivia; send them on the way with a blessing if that is appropriate.

Choose as your helper someone who is discreet, spiritually minded and always ready to oblige, though do not over work them.

Willingly carry out any guidance given to you which fosters devotion.

A mind prepared for red martyrdom (physical death).

A mind fortified and steadfast for white martyrdom (voluntary renunciation of home).

Forgiveness from the heart for everyone.

Constant prayers for those who trouble you.

Fervour in singing the order of prayer for the dead, as if every deceased faithful believer was a particular friend of yours.

Stand up when you sing hymns in honour of departed souls.

Let your vigils be constant, from evening to evening, and under the direction of another person.

Three labours in the day—prayers, work, and reading.

Divide your work into three parts: 1). the work that needs to be done in your own place; 2). the work of your brother; 3). helping your neighbours in practical ways such as making clothes and study.

Give money or goods to others as your first priority.

Do not eat until you are hungry.

Do not sleep until you are tired.

If you are given something, such as food or clothing, give something to someone who needs it.

Love God with all your heart and strength. Love your neighbour as yourself.

Live in the Old and New Testaments at all times.

You will know that you are really praying or working if tears come; or, if tears don't come freely, if you perspire.[157]

Those who became Christians in Celtic lands were inspired by stories of Christians in the Roman Empire who, because they refused to renounce Christ and swear loyalty to Roman gods, allowed themselves to be bled to death by the Roman authorities. These were known as martyrs, which means witnesses. They witnessed to Christ even if it meant death. Many Christians wanted to be all-out, like those early martyrs, but by the fifth century these persecutions had ceased. They hit on an ingenious idea. They called these Roman witnesses "red martyrs", because they shed blood, and they suggested that certain people in their day could be known as "white martyrs". These were people who gave up their life by leaving their home and things they held most dear in order to be pilgrims for the love of God in another land. The Irish adopted this with enthusiasm. These pilgrims for the love of God wandered all over the world. We shall never know how many ended their lives at the bottom of the ocean. Historians say these pilgrims contributed more to the transformation of Europe during what were known as "the Dark Ages" than any other group.[158]

The majority of people had to stay at home, however. The Irish came up with a third kind of martyr—someone who renounced their comfort zones by living alone with God in some place set apart. Some of these people were full-time hermits, but ordinary Christians took up the idea of keeping three periods of Lent, during which they would give up home comforts and spend extra time with God for days or weeks. These homeland ascetics have been called "green martyrs", but the Irish word is "*glas*". This can be translated as "green", but among early Christians it often referred to the bluey-green of death, because they put to death their own wishes. So it might be more accurate to call them "blue martyrs". *The Cambrai Homily*, a sixth or seventh-century Irish homily, so-called because it is kept in the municipal library of the French town of Cambrai, describes these three forms of martyrdom. It is one of the few surviving written sources for Old Irish in the period 700 to 900.[159]

In the English Church, Cuthbert stands as an ikon for a person who can hold pastoral, administrative and episcopal posts, and yet live a monastic life of prayer and spend nine years as an island hermit. Following the departure of the Irish and the end of the Irish Mission after the 664 Synod of Whitby, Cuthbert, who accepted the new regulations for the sake of the unity of the Church, was appointed prior of the Lindisfarne monastery. Then began the hard grind of revising the Rule to accommodate other regulations from the Continent. The *Life of Saint Cuthbert* by an anonymous monk at Lindisfarne states that "Cuthbert dwelt (at Lindisfarne) also according to Holy Scripture, following the contemplative amid the active life, and he arranged our rule of life which we composed then and which we observe to this day along with the rule of St Benedict." Sometime later, then, Cuthbert died (687), but before the 793 Viking invasion elements of the Benedictine Rule were introduced to the Saxons at Lindisfarne.

We can only guess at the contents of Cuthbert's Rule, and it is a fair guess that it reflected something of Cuthbert's character:

> His discourse was pure and frank, full of gravity and probity, full of sweetness and grace, dealing with the ministry of the law, the teaching of the faith, the virtue of temperance, and the practice of righteousness . . . He followed the example of the saints, fulfilling the duty of peace among the brothers; he held fast to humility also and the excellent gift of love without which every other virtue is worth nothing. He cared for the poor, fed the hungry, clothed the naked, took in strangers, redeemed captives, and protected widows and orphans.[160]

Some written Irish monastic rules from the eighth century onwards have survived. *The Celtic Monk: Rules & Writings of Early Irish Monks* provides us with several eighth-century Irish rules which include some practical guidance, though they do not set out an ordered basis for community.[161]

Columba belonged to the Second Order of Irish Saints (the holy presbyters) and his community essentially followed the practices of the Irish Church of that time.

On Iona, the elderly monks prayed five or six times in church, repeating all the Psalms in one day; but those of working age laboured on the land. They all joined together each evening for prayer. Holy Communion was celebrated on Sundays and festival days. These folk were free in spirit to respond to fresh circumstances: Columba would sometimes summon the brothers to pray in the night when, for example, he sensed a pilgrim was in danger.

Columbanus advised Christians to think of themselves as guests of the earth, and as perpetual pilgrims from their birth to their death. Celtic Christians who went into exile from home comforts and served God elsewhere for the rest of their lives were also known as *peregrini*.

It seems clear from the texts that the deserts of Egypt and the "deserts" of Celtic lands accommodated people of varied personality types. Some were dour and may have bordered on the masochistic, but others were outgoing and loved life. Rowan Williams's little classic illustrates how the Holy Spirit fell like dew upon the non-communicative Arsenius in one boat and equally upon the hospitable and chatty Moses, the former Ethiopian bandit, in a different boat.[162]

A similar diversity of temperament emerges in the story of Moling at Glendalough. He missed meals in order to pray in the church. He despised music as well as food, until a young man arrived and asked if he could play his harp to the brothers while they were in the refectory. They welcomed this. Since Moling, who was praying in church, missed this, the young man went to the church to play. Moling, who was kneeling in prayer, took from his pocket two balls of wax and stuffed them in his ears. The young man smiled and continued playing. To Moling's amazement, the wax in his ears began to melt. Try as he might to push it back into his ears, it just trickled down under his habit. At that moment the young man took a stone and started to scrape the harp. Moling found this excruciating sound unbearable. Then the young man threw the stone away and played music so sweet that Moling was filled with a joy greater than he had ever known. When the harpist had finished playing, Moling asked him: "Are you a devil sent to tempt me or an angel sent to bless me?" "You must make your own judgement," the young man replied. "When I scraped the harp, it made the noise of the devil, and when I played it with my fingers, it made the sound of an angel. Music, like food and drink, can be an agent of evil or a source of goodness." From that day Moling welcomed all musicians to play at the monastery, and he gave up undue fasting, abstaining from food only on those days when everybody fasted. His brothers could not help noticing that from that day he even acquired a sense of humour!

Petroc (d. 564), who had a ministry mainly in Devon and Cornwall, and founded his main monastery at Padstow, displays a serious, but not pre-programmed, approach to penance. One story suggests that he prophesied to some pilgrims that they would have no rain, but it did in fact rain. He was so mortified that he was a false prophet that as penance he left his beloved homeland for a long pilgrimage abroad. What an antidote to the spreading of fake news!

In materially "developed" countries obesity, addictions and fake celebrity spread like epidemics. Only a few forego the indulgent lifestyle that causes these in order to gain some brief prize in sport or showbiz. The internet age has locked people behind their screens: it has not become a place of rapture but a place of hell. "Tech makers have designed platforms and devices that steal our attention, distract us from our higher goals, and divide us into ideological echo chambers," wrote Jonnie Wolf in *The Observer Review* on 28 April 2019. The more we digitalize the more we crave the real. Among religions only Buddhists are thought to offer an antidote—the practice of mindfulness and detachment. The daily disciplines that Celtic Christianity transports from the desert into our living rooms are a seminal, life-saving way of life. They are an expression of mindfulness. The fruits of penance are hospitality, a just society and a loving personality.

Even in democracies prison conditions have broken down to such an extent that drug addiction, theft and violence towards fellow prisoners and staff have in places gotten out of control. At the level of crime prevention these penances instilled in a population order, decency, honesty, avoidance of abuse and a sense of God to whom they had to give account. Many of the penances were designed to bring contrition of heart and restitution that restored a broken relationship.

Although we would not impose the same forms of penance today, the principle behind them of making restitution to the person wronged in order to restore relationship is vital for our society. Restorative justice is increasingly recognized as an essential tool.

Restorative justice today brings those harmed by crime or conflict and those responsible for the harm into communication, enabling everyone affected by a particular incident to play a part in repairing the harm and finding a positive way forward. Restorative practice can be used anywhere to prevent conflict, build relationships and repair harm by enabling people to communicate effectively and positively. Restorative practice is increasingly being used in schools, children's services, workplaces, hospitals, communities and the criminal justice system.

I witnessed the final day of a restorative justice course in a prison called Sycamore Tree. It is taught in prisons in groups of up to twenty learners by Prison Fellowship volunteers. Prisoners on the programme explore the effects of crime on victims, offenders and the community, and discuss what it would mean to take responsibility for their personal actions. Some of those who had completed the course read out letters they had written to their victims which acknowledged their crime, showed awareness of the harm they had done, and asked for forgiveness.

A key for our world is to make restorative justice a common practice in families, schools and churches. Schools have divorced learning from the gut. It has been reduced to the ticking of boxes that produce the desired types to work in a consumer society. That has always undermined true wellbeing. Now that robots can do many jobs, that approach becomes doubly redundant.

Let the schoolchildren and prisoners daily practice the rhythm of deep breathing. Breathe out anger, breathe in forgiveness from the heart. Let the anger be placed in an imaginary space rocket that removes it from our stratosphere. Let forgiveness be placed in the heart of the One who forgave the human race as he was executed on a cross of wood. Breathe out gluttony—everything that weighs us down for no good reason: breathe in alertness. Breathe out greed: breathe in generosity. Breathe out "couldn't care less": breathe in dedication. Breathe out grumbling: breathe in appreciation. Breathe out envy; breathe in affirmation of our true self. Breathe out pride: breathe in encouragement of others.

A revival of dispersed ascetics may also be a key to the future of Christianity in an age of mass social media.

Hermits dotted the countryside of Britain and Ireland from earliest times. Although in today's multi-choice world few people can insulate themselves as uniformly as did those early hermits, it is noteworthy how many writers and innovators, as well as people with religious vocations, describe how they have lived solitary lives for quite long periods. I myself lived on the Holy Island of Lindisfarne for twenty-four years. I was sometimes involved with our retreat house and with travelling, but when people asked for a job description I said: "I am a part-time hermit on a part-time island." The very ebb and flow of this tidal island is a symbol of this way of life, which David Adam's poem, printed in *Holy Island Times*, captures. I myself lived on the Holy Island of Lindisfarne for twenty-four years. I was sometimes involved with our retreat house and with travelling, but when people asked for a job description I said 'I am a part-time hermit on a part-time island'. The very ebb and flow of this tidal island is a symbol of this way of life, as David Adams' poem "Ebb tide, Full tide" illustrates. He, like others, points out that there are times when we need to be like an island, and times when we need to be connected to the mainland.

David Runcorn left behind jobs as a busy parish priest, and conference and ministry development director, to experiment with hermit living because he is "captivated by a profound, compelling and ancient faith that now urgently seeks new ways of being present to an exciting, inquisitive and restless culture, impulsively adrift from any spiritual roots and unable to recognize its perils".[163] This adrift culture needs people who take time to live with God alone as much as did the second-hand religious culture of fourth-century cities.

Wendy Davies concludes that "monastic practice was well established in Wales by the early sixth century" and that this reflected aspects of Roman civic organization that the Romano-British had maintained following the departure of the Roman armies.[164] These were organized on a diocesan basis and were subject to the pillorying of Gildas in his Jeremiah-like tirade against the British church, *The Ruin of Britain*. As I indicated in chapter two, St Patrick also set up monastic churches in Ireland on the Roman model of dioceses. The renewal came through ascetical semi-hermits who embraced a more authentic form of monastic life. They wished to live for God alone, according to a rule of life. Bede tells us that many Irish monks came to instruct the English children, as well as their seniors, not only in studies, but also in the observance of the discipline of a Rule.[165]

The underlying truth of voluntary Celtic penance adopted by ascetics is that sin is a sickness of the heart and that the cure is radical applications of love of God and of one's neighbour. We must breathe into the Church the monastic disciplines or the churches will become froth or die away.

Critics of penance forget that if we are not at one with God, we become addicts to false substitutes. Penitential exercises have a similar purpose to the Twelve Steps programmes for people who are addicted to alcohol, drugs or sex. The difference is that these early Celts recognized that we are all addicts to something, whether it be pride or rage. That is why I titled my book on voluntary disciplines *The Joy of Spiritual Fitness*.[166]

Some versions of Christianity would have those who are saved dispense the Gospel to those who are lost in such a way that they lose their own humanity and fail to recognize that which is of God in the lost. Christianity becomes something a person possesses. Those who follow the Aidan and Hilda Way of Life see their life and their faith in terms of a pilgrimage. On a pilgrimage we leave behind the externals we possess and find ourselves on an equal footing with everyone else who travels; or, as someone has said, we become like a beggar who tells another beggar where we have found food.

This understanding is rooted in the nature of Christ, who "had nowhere to lay his head" (Luke 9:58). It reminds us of God's constant pleas to the ancient Israelites, once they had settled in their own land, never to forget that they were once wandering Bedouin and that they are called for all time to walk humbly with their God. Yet we see over and again in the story of both the Israelites and the Christian Church the tendency to become possessive, controlling and immoveable.

The call to become life-long pilgrims is not unique to the Celtic tradition, but it is modelled by the Irish *peregrini* in a way which etches itself upon communal memory and is surely unsurpassed in its almost reckless abandon to God's will. A guardian says to those who take life vows (The Long Voyage) in the Community of Aidan and Hilda: "In our commitment to live wholeheartedly as life-long disciples of Jesus Christ within the Community of Aidan and Hilda we follow the example of Celtic *peregrini* who were called into permanent exile from many things they held most dear and journeyed wherever God led. God calls you to leave behind anything that comes between you and God . . . "

This perhaps represents a return to the early years when the Church was known as the Way and Christians were disciples, learners, on that Way. It also marks a rediscovery of the essential part that sin and repentance have to play for real, fallible people in the growth into holiness. This contrasts with the disconnection that had developed between what people were actually like—sinners—and what they should have been like in theory after baptism—holy.

Dispersed new monastics linked by a Rule find new ways to become present to a culture adrift from its spiritual roots.

Contemporary Rules which restore daily and seasonal rhythms of prayer, work and recreation in the lives of ordinary people stand on their own merit and on biblical foundations, but they echo the rhythms of prayer that in Celtic lands were open to and pervaded all. A Rule can be legalistic. A Way is a pattern that is life-giving. A Rule is a means to an end. The end is the vision of God.

Jesus did not build his movement on the back of the Pharisees, he built it on the back of John the Baptist's movement. On the one hand Jesus took pains to explain to sincere followers ways in which his life and work fitted in to ancient ideas. It is generally assumed that some of these connections Jesus made with the Old Covenant are reflected in the public speeches of apostles that are recorded in the early chapters of the Acts of the Apostles. On the other hand, he did not let assumptions that nothing outside the tradition was valid deter him from carrying out new things that he felt the Father was giving him to do. He was clear that "new wine requires new wine skins". Christians in the Celtic tradition today regard it as axiomatic of that tradition that we listen to God and carry out fresh expressions of the divine will.

CHAPTER 11

Humanity's home is the communion of loves in the heart of God

The narrative I promote is that in the Celtic tradition, as in the East, the Trinity is a love affair. God is community, and we are to reflect that community in our lives, our churches and our society. In contrast, the Western Church has too often reduced the Trinity to a clinical doctrine, and in popular usage, to the heresy of subordinationism. That is, God the Father is the Top Person, Christ is No. 2, his lieutenant, and the Spirit is No. 3, their PR person who communicates to the world.

What is the answer to those who maintain that there is no evidence that Celtic Christianity has a distinctive understanding of the Trinity?

It is true that documentation is fragmentary. There is, however, one massive fact: when most of the rest of the Church in Europe went over to the heresy of Bishop Arius that Christ was not God, the Church in Celtic lands stayed true to the Trinity. Bishop Athanasius, who as a deacon made a proposal at the Council of Nicea that led to the promulgation of the Nicene Creed, commended the Celtic churches for this. Pelagius, the earliest well-known British theologian, wrote *De Fide Trinitates*, which refuted Arianism. The remaining fragments of this are contained in Migne's *Patrologiae Cursus Competus: Series Graeca*. We are left to speculate as to why this was so. We know that Bishop Hilary of Poitiers, like Athanasius, was exiled for remaining true to the Trinity, and that after his restoration he worked closely with Martin, who went to Tours and whose community inspired new faith communities in Britain and Ireland.

Irenaeus (d. 202), bishop of the influential Celtic-speaking church at Lyons, taught people to visualize the Trinity as a human being with both arms stretched out in love to the world: the main body was like the Father, the right arm was like Christ, the left arm was like the Spirit. Through his mentor Bishop Polycarp, Irenaeus had a direct line to the Beloved John who discipled Polycarp. We know that Celtic churches, certainly the Columba family of churches, had a special affinity with the Gospel of John, who reveals the heart of the Trinity in his Jesus dialogues of John chapters 14–17. (Bede records how the Irish argued at the Synod of Whitby that they took their tradition from John's teaching to all the churches in the East.)

The English translation of Eastern teaching to describe the Oneness of the Three Persons of the Trinity is "essence". In the Latin-speaking West, the English translation is "substance". Debates raged as to whether Christ was the same substance or of similar substance. Arguments about this or that Latin word made the Trinity seem like a doctrine removed from the flow of real life.

Then dualism entered the Western Church. Human beings were divorced from God because of their sin. God the Father was presented as the Creator. God's rescue plan was to send Jesus to suffer the penalty for human sin—so he was divorced from the Father. The Holy Spirit came at Pentecost but seems absent at crucial times before that. A split in the psyche of both Roman and Reformed Western Christianity has brought dire repercussions in its wake. The presentation of the Trinity in the Latin West got bogged down in formal propositions that lost the spirit of the original insights. Over the centuries, subordinationism crept in. In an imperial mind-set, it seemed reasonable to present the Father as the top Person. Increasing numbers of serious theologians are pointing out the need for this split to be healed. A true and whole understanding of the Trinity is fundamental to the future wellbeing of Christianity on this earth.

In contrast, in the Johannine and Eastern tradition, the Father, Son and Spirit are eternally communing with each other, are eternally within every human being and within the cosmos. Sin grieves them and causes fragmentation, but they are always within us.

A phrase in the Welsh book *Taliesin*, named after the sixth-century Brythonic poet, includes the line "Beautiful, too, is covenant with the Trinity." This phrase captures the sense of a relationship with the Triune

God. Taliesin is one of the five British bards of renown who is believed to have sung at the courts of at least three Brythonic kings.[167]

The "Creed of St Patrick" takes the universal Trinitarian Creed agreed by the Council of Nicea but adds flesh to the bones. For example, it adds these words: "he has a Son coeternal with himself, like to himself; not junior is Son to Father, nor Father senior to the Son. And the Holy Spirit breathes in them; not separate are Father and Son and Holy Spirit." Máire B. de Paor argues that Patrick is copying the text of the creed from a Gallican source because he wants his readers to understand his mission in the light of his belief in the Trinity. He is in touch with Gaul, Spain and Pannonia, the milieu of Martin of Tours. De Paor writes: "His testimony to his faith in the Trinity, which is the very kernel of our Patrician heritage, finds pithy expression in one of the best-loved prayers in honor of the Blessed Trinity from Penal Days: 'The Light of lights, the vision of the Trinity, and the grace of patience in the face of injustice.'"[168] Other commentators have pointed out that the words with which his creed ends, " . . . whom we confess and adore, one God in the Trinity of the Sacred Name", declines to use the plural ("Names") for God, since God is One. Patrick, unconfused by Arian teaching, insists that Christ "always existed with the Father" and was "begotten before the beginning of anything".[169]

The Tripartite Life 1:185 has a gloss on Psalm 68:29. This merely states: "Because of your temple at Jerusalem kings bear gifts to you." The glossator, however, makes two inferences: first, that this points to the magi who brought gifts to the infant Christ, and second, that it points us to "the birth whereby he was born of the Father before every element . . . for as the sun is prior to the day, and it is the day that makes clear everything, so the birth of the Son from the Father is prior to every element".

Ireland's greatest theologian, John Scotus Eriugena (d. 877), writes in his *Homily on the Prologue to the Gospel of John* that John

> enters the God who deifies him . . . he entered into the secret of the one essence in three substances . . . Behold the heavens open and the mystery of the most high and holy Trinity and Unity revealed to the world! . . . The Father is the Principle or beginning

from which all things were made; while the Son is the Principle
through whom all things were made . . . Whoever speaks emits
breath in the word that he utters; so, too God the Father, at one
and the same time, gives birth to the Son and, by the birth of the
Son, produces the Spirit . . . In him, as the divine voice says, we
live and move and have our being (Acts 17:28).

Oliver Davies points out in *Celtic Spirituality* that the earliest example of
the poetic tradition contains a reference to the Holy Trinity. One of the
four documents Thomas O'Loughlin includes under "Theology" in this
volume is a Welsh language text:

'The Food of the Soul' (probably mid thirteenth century). The
third part of this is a vision of the Trinity. This text combines
mystical insights into Divine beauty. It begins 'Let praise and
glory be sung—a hymn to the Trinity, Unity, One Divinity, Let
marvelous rejoicing be given—together To father, Son and Spirit
of splendor.' This text names the roots of human passions that
attach themselves to creatures or things other than God and then
examines how the opposite virtues to these vices may grow. It
locates the source of 'this blessed and affectionate love as the
Holy Trinity of Heaven . . . since all things are contained by these
three' . . .

It tells of a friar who fell into a trance while praying to the Trinity. He
saw the sky part and reveal a brilliant sun of immense splendour. On
its highest part it could be brilliant or dark as it wished, and this filled
people with fear. On its left was a radiant flame, fair, slow and lovely,
which conveyed the burning light between the sun and its rays. On the
right side of the sky the sun rays shone brightly and illumined the whole
world. The friar was told that the sun was the unity of the Three Persons
of the Trinity. The highest shining is the Father, the radiant flame is the
Holy Spirit, and the brilliant ray on the right is the Son of God.

It argues that the Trinity has a secret name: Alpha and Omega. A
(Alpha) is a triangular letter with the Father at one point, the Son at the
second, and the Spirit at the third who conveys "the affectionate love"

between them. O (Omega) is a circle which has neither beginning nor end and is present everywhere. From the tender love which flames between the Persons comes the sparks of the Church Triumphant, from where they pass to the Church Militant here below. The Trinity is a fire of love that reveals personhood. This tract contains a hymn which includes these words:

> The outpouring of our splendid praise
> Sings a song, blood without a word:
> To a communion of Three Persons
> Of everlasting unity is made. Amen.[170]

After studying the early Welsh texts, Oliver Davies concludes that the distinctively Welsh tradition can be summed up in three terms: "It is Trinitarian, Incarnational and cosmic." He notes that "it is a form of Christianity which affords a special value to the creativity of the poet".[171]

The earliest example of this poetic tradition, written in Welsh, contains a reference to the Holy Trinity. This poem was found in the margin of the ninth-century Latin *Juvencus* manuscript kept in the University Library at Cambridge. Of the nine verses, six are explicitly Trinitarian, though in different ways. This emphasis on the Holy Trinity is continued in several of the poems included in *The Black Book of Carmarthen*, possibly dating from the ninth and tenth centuries.

Belief affects behaviour. The Celtic awareness of God as the communion of the Three in One resulted in an emphasis on community. This was expressed in the monastic movement which pre-dated Patrick in Ireland and also took root in Wales from an early period.

The *Altus Prosator*, which many scholars conclude was probably written by Columba himself, begins: "The High Creator, the Unbegotten Ancient of Days, was without origin of beginning, limitless . . . with whom is the only-begotten Christ, and the Holy Spirit, co-eternal in the everlasting glory of divinity. We do not confess three gods, but say one God, saving our faith in three most glorious Persons . . . " And it continues: "By the singing of hymns . . . by thousands of angels . . . the Trinity is praised in eternal threefold exchanges."[172] This makes clear that

Columba did not separate Jesus from the Father, in the way a No. 2 is separate from the Boss.

Esther De Waal writes:

> Here is a profound experience of God from a people who are deeply Trinitarian without any philosophical struggle about how that is to be expressed intellectually. Perhaps the legend of St. Patrick stooping down to pick up the shamrock in order to explain the Trinity is after all more significant than we might have thought. It is as though he were saying to those early Irish people: Your God is a God who is Three-in-One and this is the most natural and immediately accessible thing in the world.[173]

This innate homing in on the Trinity was brought to Anglo-Saxon England. Taking his information from Sigfrid, a monk from Jarrow who had trained under Boisil, the Abbot of Melrose and the mentor of St Cuthbert, Bede (d. 735) tells us that the saint was a man of sublime virtues as well as an eminent scholar who talked constantly of the blessed Trinity.

The image of three in one is found frequently in Celtic art and poetry. Analogies from nature and daily life permeate the Celtic poems about the Trinity:

> Three folds of the cloth, yet only one napkin is there,
> Three joints of the finger, but still only one finger fair,
> Three leaves of the shamrock, yet no more
>   than one shamrock to wear,
> Frost, snow-flakes and ice, all water their origin share,
> Three Persons in God; to one God alone we make prayer.[174]

Alexander Carmichael records a range of affectionate Trinitarian prayers in his *Carmina Gadelica*, some of which I quote in *Exploring Celtic Spirituality*:

> The Three who are over my head,
> The Three who are under my tread,
> The Three who are over me here,

The Three who are over me there,
The Three who are in the earth near,
The Three who are up in their air,
The Three who in heaven do dwell,
The Three in the great ocean swell,
Pervading Three, O be with me.
Father cherish me,
Son cherish me.
Spirit cherish me,
Three all-kindly.

In his introduction to *Celtic Spirituality*, Oliver Davies writes that features in Celtic spirituality such as God's incarnation in the physical, ascetic and sacramental practices, creativity and empowering images of women "find a unity in the centrality of the doctrine of the Trinity, which profoundly shaped the religious imagination of the early Celtic peoples". He speculates that this may have been helped by their pre-Christian fascination with triads and the number three. In the twelfth century, Gerald of Wales comments on the enduring Welsh obsession with the number three and the early Irish myth and art is full of triads, trefoils and triple figures.[175]

I was reminded of this when I spoke to a post- and pre-Christian spirituality network that meets annually on Iona. We drew up a list of things about which they and "Celtic" Christians were angry with the Church. Then I proposed certain insights that I thought "Celtic Christianity" could offer. Speaking like a fool, I eulogized the Trinity. They were fascinated. One person said this made sense to him as an engineer because it was rooted in threes. A quantum physicist was also drawn to this Trinitarian dimension. She told me how a photon in the UK that was cut in half could feel the pain of the other half in Brazil. They could be separate but one.

Human beings are social animals. We find our identity in groups. Our sinful tendencies turn these groups into "us and them". The rise of globalism has led to an increase in tribalism. Factions and hate crimes increase. This cannot be cured by unreal liberal politics. Human groups have to find the security of a home. Only if we find our home in God can "us and them" be turned into "we". *Deus, ergo sum*: If God, I am. If Trinity: we are.

Bishop Martin Wallace[176] writes:

> I find helpful and therapeutic the drawing of the symbol of the
> Trinity, seeing the symbol reminds me of how interdependent
> they are, and how we need to be daily incorporating the Trinity,
> the Father, Son, and Holy Spirit into our daily lives. If you believe
> it or not, they are interested and are desiring us to be co-creators
> with them. We have been invited to be part of their community,
> so we are not alone. God is with us in every area of our lives
> and desires to be with us. If we but allow them in, by giving the
> invitation, and welcome them to be with us, in all aspects of our
> lives.

It is hard to be drawn into the heart of a hierarchy but easy to be drawn
into the heart of a relationship. If we are made in the image of God, we are
made to be in community. The result of mutual surrender and reciprocal
communion is community.

Polls reveal a sharp decline in religious belief in Europe and North
America. Hand in hand with that decline is a decline in values such as
truth, goodness and justice. The theory of evolution led many to assume
that since neither humans nor other creatures were created by God, the
survival of the fittest is the primary law of society. Liberalism was based
on the concept of freedom, which had to be protected against oppressive
governments and institutions. It is now claimed that humans inherit fears,
hatreds, biases and craving that they do not choose, and that artificial
intelligence can hack into these, push the emotional buttons and reap rich
rewards for social media capitalists who are out of control.

This does not mean that people have stopped believing. Everyone
believes in something. It means that the Selfie replaces God, and Me First
replaces the Common Good. But after a generation, to make our home
in Selfishness becomes hell. Society disintegrates.

The key that can turn things round is the realization that our common
home is the eternal communion in the heart of God, which we are
designed to reflect. If God is a clockmaker up there, watching the clock
of creation tick away, of course people disbelieve in such a god. But if God
is eternally birthing, including our cosmos, and accompanying the whole

messy process from the inside, we are not prisoners of a meaningless chaos. The Celtic grasp of this dimension can turn our culture round. Pelagius understood that we all inherit tendencies and imbibe influences. That is why he inculcated the practice of constant reflection on our impulses, and the possibility and responsibility we have to make good choices. All people need an affirmation in order to do this. If God is our home, everyone may find that affirmation, however much they have been abused.

Penny Warren, Members' Guardian of the Community of Aidan and Hilda, wrote in *The Aidan Way:*

> I AM is the perfect example of Simplicity.
>
> When a crowd came to arrest Jesus in the Garden, led by one of his closest colleagues who was to betray him, and accompanied by another close colleague, Peter, reacting with violence, there was a cocktail of confusion in actions, dynamics and emotions. Yet Jesus simply accepted the reality in all its pain. There was no delay, disguise, or backlash. 'Are you then he?' they asked. 'I AM' he replied 'Yahweh'. He revealed himself in the Trinity. They fell back in awe. It was utter Simplicity. Simplicity revealed God.
>
> Longing for God is the perfect example of Purity.
>
> In Rublev's ikon of the Trinity each longs for the other. This is pure longing. In this longing is their oneness.
>
> Listening with the heart is the perfect example of Obedience.
>
> Each in the Rublev Icon is depicted as listening attentively with an open heart.
>
> Too often we keep Jesus stuck as a merely earth-bound Jesus. Fasting—to put our shouting, noisy bodies to one side, cleaning out the rubbish—enables us to enter into these three qualities of the Trinity.
>
> When I share this vision of restoring God as Relationship as the heart of business, economics, family and community life people look incredulous. They point out that many people have been born of incest or of test tubes, or they have never known a parent or who their siblings are. Others have been driven by false peer pressure. Life for many is about rejection, lust or manipulation.

Where is the image of the Loving Relationship in them? Where are the Loving Three-in-One in our consumerist, individualist, fragmented societies? How may we restore consciousness of the Trinity in all this mess?

A person who works in an IVF clinic says that the meeting of sperm and egg is beautiful and divine, whoever the sperm and the egg come from. Even a person who was born of incest can find healing of the harm caused by abuse and discover the same truth. God is in their conception. They are born of the divine DNA of the eternally Loving Three, even though the human agents spurned it. Jesus said: "I go to my Father and your Father." We are bound together in the divine family.

But how may this truth come home to us and become our daily companion? Every day I rise from bed and say: "I arise today with the Father eternally in me, with Jesus eternally in me and with the Spirit eternally in me, making all through love." I let the feeling of their love flow through my body, mind and heart. And in the heat of the day, as I work in the context of an organization or network, I make an act of will: I look upon it as if it is an extended family. By faith I relate to each person as if they are part of the family that reflects the Triune Love. And as I sleep I echo those words: "I lie down with the Father eternally in me, Jesus eternally in me, the Spirit eternally in me, making all through love." Whether I live or die, the Eternal Three of Love are my home.

The Canadian Mark Carney, when he was Governor of the Bank of England in 2018, warned that the Fourth Industrial Revolution, which would be dominated by artificial intelligence, automation, bio-technology and 3D printing, would in a short time mercilessly destroy livelihoods and identities. Just as workers once had to shift from using their hands to using their heads as machines took over, so as robots take over, we will have to shift from using our heads to using our hearts. Emotional intelligence, originality and social skills such as persuasion and caring for others would come to prominence (*The Times*, 15 September 2018).

The future of Christianity and the future of the world may lie in recognition that ultimate reality is a Communion of Loves in the Heart of God, and that the purpose of human life is to reflect that on earth. This is the abiding truth at the heart of Celtic spirituality.

CHAPTER 12

A robotized world can find
communities of love

It is true that most of our sources for the early church in Celtic lands are monastic. The monasteries perhaps formed the majority of churches. They were not, however, monochrome. Like the monasteries in the East, each founder and each place had its own character.

It is true that our cyber society is vastly different from early Celtic tribal society, but paradoxically, new social fluidity has room for fresh monastic expressions that are rooted in the old.

Insula Sanctorem et Doctorum collates a huge amount of source and secondary materials to describe scores of monastic settlements in Ireland—their founders, disciplines, buildings—in the fifth, sixth and seventh centuries.[177] Hugh Graham aims to give "a critical and fairly complete account of the Irish Monastic Schools which flourished prior to 900 A.D".[178] John Ryan considers much material through a Roman Catholic lens.[179]

According to the calculations of Sir James Ware, there were 164 famous monastic schools in Ireland, but there were many more smaller ones.[180]

Many monasteries were surrounded either by a *rath* (an earth ridge) or a *cathair* (a stone wall). The inner circle of the monastery often included the church or churches, oratories, refectory, kitchen, school, a chamber for the preservation of books and literary apparatus and/or a scriptorium, a hospice or guesthouse, monks' cells, workshops or offices for the smith and the carpenter. Outside this circle were buildings for farming, milling, crafts or storage. A byre for cows was located in pastureland and there were sometimes ponds for fishing. In the early days, cells were built of earth, wattle or wood. Stone buildings began to be substituted in the eighth century. As Columbanus taught, fasting and prayer, labour and study were the daily tasks of the monk.

Ninian founded the first recorded monastic community in Britain north of the Emperor Hadrian's wall about 397, a few miles inland from the large port at what is now the Isle of Whithorn. My friend Russ Parker likes to say that Ninian built his cell at Spaghetti Junction. That is because the waterways were the motorways of those days. One cross carved in St Ninian's Cave has been carbon-dated to the 600s. Whithorn was a busy sea route between today's Wales and northern Britain. This included a church and individual monks' cells with central hearths near it. It grew to host students from far and wide, a famous library, and many fields for crops, hospitality and vellum. This was inspired by the White House of St Martin of Tours. Recent archaeological excavations indicate the original buildings. According to Daphne Brooke, archaeological evidence suggests it could have been an actual daughter house of Martin's "Big Family" (*Muintir*).[181] According to tradition, Ninian founded many cells and small monastic settlements in the north-eastern part of Britain (what is now Scotland).

On the basis of the *Lives* of the Welsh saints, Oliver Davies (1996) suggests that there were broadly three types of monasteries in western Britain (now Wales). There were major monastic centres such as Llancarfan, Tywyn, Llanbadarn Fawr, Clynnog Fawr and St Illtud's community at Llantwit Major. In addition to these large and bustling monasteries which followed a less rigorous pattern of life, there were communities where manual labour was the norm for all and which were regarded as being more ascetical in their character.

According to one tradition, Illtud's method was to combine spirit, mind and body in a harmony. He divided students into twenty-four groups, each responsible for one hour's worship and adoration, so that ceaseless praise would flow. The intellectual side involved instruction in the "seven sciences", the best knowledge the times could offer. Physical wellbeing was fostered by clearing the land, digging and ploughing. Hearing of a famine in what is now Brittany, Illtud loaded a boat with seed corn. Great future leaders such as Samson, Gildas, David and Paul Aurelian were drawn there to study.

In the Roman Empire, Christian monastic schools started to replace pagan schools in places such as Alexandria, Milan, Arles and Marseilles. Ireland became a land of schools, as part of monastic cities of God which provided all that was needed in the material and moral order.

According to the *Tripartite Life*, Patrick was schooled for a generation in the greatest pioneer monasteries of Gaul and Italy. These most likely included St Martin's at Marmoutier (Tours), Germanus's at Auxerre, Cassian's at Marseilles, and Honoratus of Arles's most famed monastery at Lerins. There, Honoratus turned a barren island into a Garden of Eden. Patrick himself was an apostle, not a monastic founder, but in the fifth century he founded his see at Armagh and recruited many monks and nuns. The "Catalogue of the Saints of Ireland" refers to this as the first missionary order. The second order were monks and nuns of the sixth century who founded great and small monastic foundations throughout Ireland. Some first trained in Britain at monasteries such as Whithorn. The two most formative of these foundation monasteries were Enda's at Aran and Finnian's at Clonard.

About 484, Enda, who became known as the "patriarch of Irish monasticism" founded a monastery on the Isle of Aran to which most of the great Christian leaders came. Enda's father was the pagan king of Oriel, in the north. His sister, Fanchea, became a nun, founded nunneries at Rossary and elsewhere, and transformed her brother from pillaging and tribal killings to radical discipleship of Christ. He trained in the sacred disciplines, probably at Whithorn in the 470s. Upon his return he persuaded the King of Munster to grant him the most westerly of the Aran Isles as a place which became known as "the home of God's saints".

There, locals who were at first hostile became Christians. He started with a monastery at Killeany. It is said he divided the island into ten parts, each with an *abba*, a church and a village with stone cells. Giants of Ireland's Christianization such as Brigid, Brendan, Finnian, Columba, Ciaran and Kevin spent time there and became founders of great monasteries. Their rule, like that of most later monasteries, was work, prayer and study. They were responsible for procuring and preparing their own food. Grave inscriptions include Romans, so presumably Roman citizens from places such as Gaul also joined them. There are more Christian remains at Aran than anywhere else in Ireland.

Finnian's monastic school at Clonard is the most celebrated, if not the first, of the great monastic centres of the sixth century. He became known as the Tutor of the Saints of Erin. Clonard is situated by the River Boyne, which divides south and north Ireland, by the Esker ridge, a key west-east route. It was a neutral place, open to all. Finnian was schooled under various saints in Ireland and Britain, including Gildas and David of Wales. He performed miracles of faith but retained poverty of spirit. In later life he founded his great monastic school at Clonard about the year 520. He began alone and lived in a simple cell of wattles and clay, then built a little church and enclosed them. He slept on the bare ground with a chain around his naked body. Like a magnet, many were attracted to live around a person of such holiness and scholarship. It was said that he trained "the twelve apostles of Ireland". These were Ciaran of Seir, Cieran of Clonmacnoise, Columba of Iona, Brendan of Clonfert, Brendan of Birr, Colman of Terryglass, Molaise of Devenish, Canice of Aghaboe, Ruadan of Lorrha, Mobi of Glasnevin, Sinnel of Cleenish and Ninnidh of Inishmacsaint.[182] All these apostles went out to found monasteries and schools that were famed throughout Europe. The so-called Office of St Finnian claims that he had 3,000 scholars under his instruction. There was no great library or hall; the teaching was all by word of mouth, and the students built their own little huts in the surrounding meadows, where they fished and milled their grain. Monks spent hours with their hands spread in prayer, in study of Scripture, and in manual labour.

As we have noted, Brigid founded a monastery for women and men at Kildare about 490. As years passed her festival became second only to that of Patrick himself and she became known as one of Ireland's three patron saints. Although many sources refer to St Brigid, the first ordered *Life* is a quite late collection of stories by Bishop Cogitosus, an eighth-century monk at Kildare. Sources include "A Hymn to Brigid" by her uncle, the monk Ultan, who often had 200 orphans whom he personally fed; a seventh-century hymn by St Brogan; an equally ancient Latin hymn which names Brigid as "Mary of the Gael"; and five *Lives*, collected and printed by the Irish Franciscan friar John Colgan in Louvain in 1647. These are variously attributed to an unknown monk Animosus, a twelfth-century English monk Laurence of Durham, and a monk from the holy island of Lough Derg who flourished in the eighth century, found in a Monte Cassino library.

Brigid built her first cell under an oak ("dara") tree, and hence called that place Cell-Dara. It grew quickly into two monasteries, one for women and one for men. We learn that they grew apples, made ale, gave hospitality to the poor, and healed the sick. Bishop Conleath, who led the men's monastery, was an expert craftsman in metal, and made many chalices and bells. Perhaps somewhat less ascetic than the monasteries of Brigid's male predecessors, zeal for prayer, good works and hospitality flourished, a large church was built that could accommodate the many who flocked there, and monks and nuns developed artistic skills and crafts.

Monasteries were founded at Monasterboice and Cluainfois about 500. William Reeves compiled a list of more than a hundred monasteries founded by or dedicated to Columba—thirty-seven in Ireland, thirty-two among the Scots, thirty-two among the Picts. These included Derry, Durrow, Kells and Iona in Britain.[183] Molaise founded Devenish about 530, Senan (who founded monasteries in the estuaries of rivers) founded Scattery about 537, and another Finnian founded Moville about 540. Ciaran founded Clonmacnoise about 544. Brendan was tutored by Bishop Erc and by St Ita, "the foster mother of the saints of Ireland", at her "nursery for saints" at Killeady. Following his two heroic voyages across the ocean, he built numerous cells in his home area around Brandon to accommodate the many who were inspired to follow his monastic way of life. Then he founded Clonfert about 553. It was said that he schooled 3,000. Glendalough monastery grew up around followers of Kevin.

Bangor monastery was established by St Comgall in 558. Bangor was a major centre of learning—called the "Light of the World"—and trained many missionaries. Carthach of Lismore and Fintan of Doon studied there. St Mirin was a prior at Bangor before leaving to found Paisley Abbey in Renfrewshire. Columbanus and Gall went off to continental Europe in 590 and founded the famous monasteries of Luxeuil (France), St Gallen (Switzerland) and Bobbio (Italy).

The 3,000 brothers at Bangor ensured that it became known as a place of perennial praise. Worship groups maintained music 24/7 on a rota basis. A musical student at Bangor, who accompanied Columbanus to the Continent, was Gall. When he died in 645, the fame of his monastic school in the Swiss town now named after him had spread far and wide. In 870, an Irish brother named Moengal was appointed Head of the Music School at St Gall. Hymns were composed by Irish poets such as Sedulius, Dungal, Sechnall, Columba, Molaise, Cuchuimne, Columbanus, Ultan, Colman, Cummian, Aengus, Fiacc, Brodan, Sanctan and Moelisu.[184] Summarizing the history of Irish music up to the close of the ninth century, W. H. G. Flood writes:

> The Irish had . . . battle marches, dance tunes, folk songs, chants and hymns in the fifth century; they were the earliest to adopt the neums of plainchant of the Western Church; they modified and introduced Irish melodies into the Gregorian Chant; they had an intimate acquaintance with the diatonic scale . . . . They were the first to employ harmony and counterpoint, they had quite an array of bards and poets; they employed blank verse, elegiac and . . . rhymes . . . laments, elegies, metrical romances etc; they had a world-famed school of harpers, and finally they diffused music knowledge over Europe.[185]

Within the extensive rampart which encircled Bangor's monastic buildings, students studied Scripture, theology, logic, geometry, arithmetic, music and the classics. Mo Sinu moccu Min was the fifth abbot of Bangor. It is thought that he tutored Columbanus.

Gilbert Markus claims that the whole of Irish society was status-conscious and cites evidence of the hierarchical nature of Celtic churches. The *Uraicecht na Riar* says that poets have seven grades and three sub-grades, and the Irish laws discuss the different grades of clergy, their rights and honour.[186] This mostly pertained to the diocesan system, which over the centuries grew stronger. Celtic monasteries were not without their faults. To begin with, in Ireland, the abbots were chosen from within the tribe's ruling family, though most of them were open to the poor and abbas had soul friends from other places. However, the eighth-century Celi De reform movement ended hereditary leadership. The key element about their monasteries was that they were built on ascetic practices that rooted out possessiveness and cover-ups. There is not one hint of child abuse in the accounts of Irish or British monasteries.

Although it is generally agreed that many tribes had their own home-grown church, and that there were monastic families of churches which each had some distinctive characteristics, some trans-tribal characteristics that were strong in Celtic lands are also apparent. For example, the influence of the Desert Fathers and Mothers, the passion for the three forms of martyrdom (red, green and white), the love of learning and hospitality.

De Paor gives a sense of how open and hospitable of spirit these devout religious were to one another. Darerca sets out to stay with and learn from Ibar, in the full expectation that she will be warmly received:

> Therefore the virgin of Christ, placing her trust in the Lord, set out. Along with the eight other virgins and the widow—together with some others—to make her way to the reverend pontiff Ibar, who was settled in the western islands of Ireland; for that is what she had longed to do. When St Darerca with her company reached the man of God, she spent a long time under his rule with many other virgins.[187]

De Paor also tells of Darerca's visit to St Brigid, who is equally accessible to her.

Although many monasteries were tribal, the best of them were free from what we might call nationalism. Their rule of hospitality inspired them to welcome people from other races and lands. Bede comments that in the 660s:

> There were many English nobles and lesser folk in Ireland who had left their own land (Britain) during the episcopates of Bishops Finan and Colman, either to pursue religious studies or to lead a life of stricter discipline. Some of these soon devoted themselves to the monastic life, while others preferred to travel, studying under various teachers in turn. The Irish welcomed them all kindly, and without asking for payment, provided them with daily food, books, and instruction.[188]

The archaeological surveys of the monastic remains at Nendrum, in Northern Ireland, reveal three concentric circles. The innermost circle is a place of prayer. The second circle housed things such as a school. The outer circle, so some guides suggest, housed workers, families and animals. This pattern is not uncommon. It indicates that all human life revolved around the monastic churches. There were different levels of commitment but all in some sense belonged.

In an article entitled "Is there an archaeology of lay people at early Irish monasteries?" Tomás Ó Carragáin argues:

> There have been major changes in recent years in our understanding of the organization of ecclesiastical power structures in Ireland. The traditional view was that early Irish churches were overwhelmingly monastic in character, but now it is recognized that only a small minority of the thousands of churches established in Ireland were monasteries in the usual sense of the term. Many of them were community or family churches served (sometimes only occasionally) by a priest, rather than by a community of monks.
>
> In the case of these fairly minor sites, it is often difficult to determine their character because of limited documentary coverage and ambiguous archaeology. The founders of the most important sites, such as Armagh and Clonmacnoise, were conceived of as ascetic monastic figures; but, whatever their initial character, most of these sites became multi-functional with a resident bishop in addition to a variety of religious communities.
>
> There is abundant documentary evidence that significant numbers of lay people spent time at ecclesiastical sites as pilgrims, penitents, patients, paupers, travellers and seekers of sanctuary. There is also documentary evidence that some lay people were buried at monastic sites and some sites feature satellite cemeteries apparently for certain sections of the laity.
>
> All extensively excavated ecclesiastical sites have produced some evidence for craft activity. An example of the latter is sculpture, which at a few sites like Clonmacnoise, was produced on quite a large scale at certain times, with the production of

many of the minor pieces (grave-slabs etc.) probably coinciding with the commissioning of monumental high crosses, especially in the ninth and early tenth centuries. Another craft particular to ecclesiastical sites is the production of vellum, which is best attested archaeologically at Portmahomack, a Pictish monastery on the east coast of Scotland excavated by Martin Carver. Rows of cattle metapodials set vertically in the ground were interpreted as pegs from a vanished wooden stretcher for preparing vellum, and there was also a lined tank for tanning leather and sea shells to produce a light colour suitable for vellum.[189]

Another common feature was the production of ecclesiastical metalwork. One of the most common items of ecclesiastical metalwork to survive in Ireland is the handbell. They are preserved in relatively large numbers because they came to be considered associative relics of the founding saints. Paul Stevens's landmark publication of his excavations at Clonfad, Co. Westmeath, has given us a stunning insight into the processes surrounding the production and distribution of such bells.[190]

Clonfad was chief church of the southern half of the kingdom of Fir Tulach. It was established in the sixth century and excavation of its eastern periphery produced features dating mainly from the sixth to the ninth century. The ironworking took the form of primary and secondary smithing, especially the manufacture of iron handbells, each of which was produced from a single large sheet of iron.

Most of the documentary evidence points to stationary workshops, but the laws make provision for the likelihood that craftspeople had to move about. The *Uraicecht Becc* stipulates that, unlike the general population, craftspeople were allowed to travel between kingdoms (*túatha*) and that they were assured of protection. A number of sections of the eighth-century *Collectio Canonum Hibernensis* refer to the payment of wages to labourers from the property of the church site.

Evidence from European monasteries founded by Irish missionaries suggests that industrial and craft activity, along with the agricultural labour, was carried out by non-monastics who were collectively referred to as a *familia*. Some of these lived within the monastery (the *familia intus*) and their accommodation is depicted on the plan of St Gall.

Some renounced their personal property and income upon entering the monastery, while others retained one or both. Unlike these, the dependents who lived on the monastery's outlying estates (the *familia foris*) could marry and raise a family.

To date, the most extensive evidence for craft activity from an Irish ecclesiastical complex comes from Clonmacnoise, especially in and around the residential area excavated by Heather King east of the main ecclesiastical complex—the New Graveyard excavations. In Hiberno-Scandinavian Dublin, plot boundaries suggest that, from the tenth century, craft-workers had some personal claim over their workshops. The absence of boundaries suggests, perhaps, that they were *manaig* (from the Latin word "*monachus*", alone, root of the English word "monk").

Important Irish churches, too, had a wide range of dependents, tenants and clients of varying status. Such ecclesiastical tenants were often married and seem to have farmed lands at a distance from the church. The terminology used for them is monastic; however, they were expected to live by relatively strict rules in what Etchingham describes as a paramonastic existence. Charles-Edwards has questioned the validity of a clear-cut distinction between monk and monastic tenant: in all likelihood we are dealing with a spectrum of categories, the boundaries between which may sometimes have been blurred.[191] They were seldom referred to as monasteries. Civitas, or cities of God, was a more widely used term.[192]

Rowan Williams argues that a church is meant to be the community of communities, while Philip Sheldrake writes:

> Monks in the tradition of Columbanus saw monastic settlements as anticipations of paradise in which the forces of division, violence and evil were excluded. Wild beasts were tamed and nature was regulated. The privileges of Adam and Eve in Eden, received from God but lost in the Fall, were reclaimed. The living out of this vision of an alternative world involved all the people who were brought within the enclosed space. It was not something that concerned merely the 'professional' ascetics. The Columbanian tradition, for example, believed that all people were called from birth to the experience of contemplation. So,

'monastic' enclosures were places of spiritual experience and non-violence and also places of education, wisdom and art. Within the enclosures there took place, ideally speaking, an integration of all the elements of human life, as well as of all classes of human society.[193]

The Fourth Industrial Revolution threatens to reduce humans to robot-users, and to reduce communities to dormitories. Western democracies are sleepwalking into a new tyranny—the untrammelled power of tech giants and social media disinformation. The infrastructure of democracy hangs by a thread. When there are trade wars and global infrastructure breaks down, we need communities that are self-sufficient, know how to live on a bare minimum and sustain bonds. My Irish nephew promotes permaculture. He tells me that two acres could feed 200 people with vegetables for a year. Chickens and five pigs each year could provide the meat. They could plant forests for building and use hemp for clothing. You can still trade in kind or by local coinage.

Faith communities of the future need to soak the locality in prayer and seek its wellbeing, understand and befriend all who serve the common good, and link networks up in a spirit of community. This, however, is not the prevalent model of church. Prayer has been privatized. Learning has been handed over to those who fail to root it in love of God and the common good. Material provision comes from mass production that violates creation. A recovery of Christian communities that combine daily corporate prayer in the rhythms of the sun, holistic learning and eco-sufficiency is imperative. Many Free Churches, and more recently my own Church of England, have adopted an activities-based mission to compensate for the loss of priestly vocations, which takes the church further downhill. What is needed is to replace this with a fostering of vocations, soul friends, spiritual practices and love of neighbourhood until the aroma of holiness and hospitality attracts new converts. In short, we need a Celtic model of church.

Three models of church are currently front-runners:

1. The institutional model: the church pays a pastor to keep members happy. This puts maintenance before God.

2. The attractional model: the church finds out what consumers want and provides attractive programmes. This puts recruitment before God.

3. The missional model: New groups make disciples and multiply. This can put the part before the whole, mission before God. ISIS and Pepsi have a mission—it is their values that determine their worth. Before God sends, God is.

What is needed is to replace this with a fostering of vocations, soul friends, spiritual practices and love of neighbourhood until the aroma of holiness and hospitality attracts new converts. In short, we need a Celtic model of church. Western culture is at a turning point. Christendom forms of church (churches organized according to the machinery and mind-set of empire) are dying, but spirituality increases. Many who seek a fresh expression of church that has deep Christian roots ask: "Is there a Celtic model for modern churches?"

We can categorize two prevalent models of early churches in Celtic lands: the cell, and the village hub. As we have seen, tribal leaders gave lands by the strategic highways of sea and river to church planters who established communities of daily prayer, education, hospitality and land care. Peoples' monastery churches served as daily prayer base, school, library, scriptorium/arts centre, drop-in and health centre. They had farms with livestock and crops, workshops such as wood, spinning and milling. They were open to the world. They offered soul friends, training and even entertainment. Children, housewives, farm workers and visitors would wander in and out. Visitors brought news from overseas. They were villages of God. Each had its own flavour in worship and values (Rule), yet each was connected with the universal church through common practices, prayers and priests ordained in the apostolic succession.

Although our society is vastly different, changing trends again require churches that are more than single-building Sunday-only congregations:

- A twenty-four-hour society calls for seven-days-a-week churches.
- A cafe society calls for churches that are eating places.
- A travelling society calls for churches that provide accommodation and reconnect with the hostel movement.

- A stressed society calls for churches that provide spaces for retreat and meditation.
- A multi-choice society calls for churches that have a choice of styles and facilities.
- A fragmented society calls for holistic models and whole life discipling.
- An eco-threatened society calls for more locally sustainable communities.

A fourth model might be termed incarnational. Christians embody and continue Christ's life and work—they make community and build God's kingdom. But because it has daily rhythms of prayer and is the hub of local community, I think it is reasonable to name this a Celtic model of church. As the heart is to a person so a Celtic church is to the community or network it serves.

It has a heart for God—sustained by daily prayer; for others—sustained by hospitality and nurture; for the world—cherishing the earth and society. It is a journeying church. In many churches the focus of time and energy is maintenance of a programme or building. This produces overload, so that any new leads from God are blocked out. In a Celtic-style church, programmes and buildings are provisional; they flow out of Spirit-led initiatives, and when that tide ebbs they are beached. A church that embraces a Celtic spirit starts its journey from where it is. It discerns which features of a village of God it can move towards on its own or with others. Some may enrich existing services with Celtic prayer patterns. Certain congregations may introduce daily prayer, a rule of life for core members and soul friends; others may relocate from an anachronistic building to a house of prayer.

A church with resources and a viable site may review which of these features of a village of God they can develop or (if their site is not a hub) link up with:

- Sacred or praying spaces
- Eating space
- Accommodation space
- Learning space

- Art space
- Wild space
- Conference space
- Recreation space
- Godly play space
- Eco space
- Shop space
- Workshop space
- Meditation space
- Wi-fi space

In many places a church building of alien style is the only obvious point of access to Christianity. A Celtic church is like the hub of a wheel with spokes that reach into work, social, educational, health, sport, business and care networks. Like yeast in dough, these gradually become part of a transforming sense of community.

These possibilities are explored in *Ancient Ways for Modern Churches*.[194]

A modern village of God starts with a church that is a hub spiritually—core members sustain a daily rhythm of prayer in different forms—and most often it starts with a church building that is a hub physically. It may be at the heart of a shopping centre, town or village. It may have multi-facilities—a café, gym, library, children's play area, youth club, exhibition area, meeting or conference rooms, for example. It hosts religious, educational and fun events. Any church can co-sponsor all kinds of things from A–Z: Arts, Boxing, Crafts, Dance, Eco-projects, Festivals, Gardens, Healing, Internet use, Jam-making, Learning, Markets, Outdoor pursuits, Pubs, Quizzes, Reading groups, Sports, Travel accommodation, Units for hire, Volunteering, Weddings, Youth work, Zimmer-frame activities. My virtual chart of a village of God continues to attract much feedback.[195] A house church in Australia urged me to add a wrestling arena, others think a cash machine is now a vital component, and a vicar explained how the vicarage is a community hub which raises money for charity by hiring the garden out for wedding celebrations! Another church in the UK has established Christians Against Poverty. This provides debt counselling for people in financial difficulty and job clubs and projects for those seeking employment.

Epilogue

It was in 1987 that philosopher Alistair McIntyre predicted a new Dark Age and called for "a new Benedict" who would be unlike the first one. Rod Dreher, a senior editor at *The American Conservative* and author of *The Benedict Option: A Strategy for Christians in a Post-Christian Nation*, argues that we are witnessing the end of Christendom.[196]

End times indeed draw near. Pandemics such as COVID-19 break out. Trade wars increase. International infrastructures break down. A rootless and egotistical globalized elite seems set to rule the world, rendering national democracies a charade. This leads to a revival of neo-fascism and tribalism. In fear, we turn to people with destructive ideas to govern us. The politics of identity takes centre stage. We become self-centred, fearful.

But Benedict is the wrong ikon for our time. Following the reports of shocking sexual abuse and institutional cover-ups over many years in English Catholicism's two most prestigious schools, Downside and Ampleforth, both run by Benedictine monasteries, a feature article in the UK's Catholic weekly *The Tablet* concludes that the UK Government's "Inquiry into Child Sexual Abuse" reveals "a culture of superiority, arrogance and insularity . . . The problems go even deeper than the particular problems of English Benedictines—as far as the sixth century rule of St. Benedict, by which the monks live. Benedict's rule reflects a patriarchal theology in which belief in an all-knowing, all-powerful God the Father is mirrored in an all-powerful male leader. This gives huge authority to the abbot—an authority which some of them have been unwilling to surrender to the police or social services, or even allow them to challenge their views or decisions . . . "[197]

Bernard, abbot of the Reformed Benedictine abbey of Clairvaux, jointly declared war on the Slav pagans (the Wends) in 1147. "The battle should not be stopped until either their rites or the natives themselves have been wiped out," he declared.[198]

The worldwide child abuse scandal has rocked the Roman Catholic and other churches to their foundations. Mary McAleese, the former President of Ireland and a lay canon lawyer, describes her church as "an empire of misogyny". This is part of a wider church crisis of corruption and loss of institutional authority. If it is to be rooted out, action needs to be taken to throw out abuses that include enforced clerical celibacy, a ban on women priests, the dismissal of Anglican Orders, and the unilateral usurpation of powers by the Bishop of Rome in 1064. This general crisis was foretold by a surprising prophet. In 1969, Joseph Ratzinger, the future Pope Benedict XVI, made a startling prophecy on German radio. Four years after the end of the Second Vatican Council, he predicted that the Catholic Church was at the beginning of a great and wide-ranging catastrophe, one that would destroy its wealth, power and status. Father Ratzinger recognized that the Church would not survive in its then-current state the cultural revolution shaking Western civilization: "From the crisis of today, the church of tomorrow will emerge—a church that has lost much," he said. "She will become small and will have to start afresh more or less from the beginning." Celtic Christianity calls all Christians to "come back to the quarry from which you were hewn" (Isaiah 51:1).

Let the Pope invite the world's bishops, following preparation, to a council to wait on the Holy Spirit: renounce his unilateral self-chosen powers, accept Anglican Orders, allow intercommunion, married priests, voluntary celibacy and women's ordination in those provinces whose culture finds this appropriate.

As the threat of a new Dark Age looms, the question becomes paramount—What are the building blocks of lasting civilization? We need fresh expressions of Celtic monasticism which have rhythms of prayer, roots in pre-schism catholicity and relationships with all branches of the universal Body of Christ. Let the world's churches pursue life-long, holistic learning.

We cannot, of course, recreate the organization of the early Celtic church, nor should we. But it is possible to learn from it. It was Archbishop Michael Ramsey, quoting Arnold Toynbee, that great historian of the rise and fall of civilizations, who distinguished between historical movements based on archaism, and those based on transfiguration. As we grasp something of the mind-set and dynamic of the Church in Celtic lands, we can move forward in a way that transforms.

—

We have explored twelve criticisms and twelve keys of Celtic Christianity. There are other elements that are seldom criticized, for example, pilgrimage and justice.

The Irish loved pilgrimage so much that some of them became "pilgrims for the love of God" who went into exile from their home comforts for the rest of their lives. These were known as white martyrs. Others became inner pilgrims for the rest of their lives and became known as green martyrs. I spent a day at Ardmore, in Ireland, with pilgrims who had walked the twelve sections of St Declan's Way over a year; they wanted to know how they could become inner pilgrims for the rest of their lives. I introduced them to the Ten Waymarks and regular spiritual practices of the Community of Aidan and Hilda.

Justice was fundamental to the foundational centuries of Celtic Christianity. They understood, in the words of Dr Martin Luther King, that "the arc of the moral universe is long, but it bends towards justice". St Patrick wrote a passionate rebuke to the soldiers of the British pirate chief Coroticus:

> The Christians of Roman Gaul have the custom of sending holy
> and chosen men to the Franks and to other pagan peoples with
> so many thousands in money to buy back the baptised who have
> been taken prisoner. You, on the other hand, kill them, and sell
> them to foreign peoples who have no knowledge of God. You
> hand over the members of Christ as it were to a brothel. What
> hope have you in God? Who approves of what you do, or whoever
> speaks words of praise? God will be the judge, for it is written:
> 'Not only the doers of evil, but also those who go along with it,
> are to be condemned'.

St Columba stood up to people who acted unjustly. Adomnan records how he prophesied over several poor, but generous, people that their cows would increase. On the other hand, he pronounced the following prophetic sentence on a certain rich and very stingy man named Uigene, who despised St Columba and showed him no hospitality, saying:

> But the riches of that niggardly man who hath despised Christ in the strangers that came to be his guests, will gradually become less from this day, and be reduced to nothing; and he himself shall be a beggar; and his son shall go about from house to house with a half-empty wallet: and he shall be slain by a rival beggar with an axe, in the pit of a threshing floor.

All this was fulfilled in both cases, according to the prophecy of the holy man.

Bede writes of Aidan in Northumbria:

> Never, through fear or respect of persons, did he keep silence with regard to the sins of the rich; but was wont to correct them with a severe rebuke. He never gave money to the powerful men of the world, but only food, if he happened to entertain them; and, on the contrary, whatsoever gifts of money he received from the rich, he either distributed, as has been said, for the use of the poor, or bestowed in ransoming such as had been wrongfully sold for slaves. Moreover, he afterwards made many of those he had ransomed his disciples, and after having taught and instructed them, advanced them to priest's orders.

Hilda of Hartlepool and Whitby taught everyone to observe strictly the virtues of justice.

The St Chad Gospels (ninth century) and the Bodmin Gospels (tenth century) furnish the first examples in the post-Roman world of people seeking to abolish slavery, with manumissions granting freedom entered into blank spaces in the text.

Justice requires a concept of truth. Democracy requires common values. Science requires a connecting narrative. The planet, threatened by the catastrophes of global warming, requires tender care. As Eros runs unchecked across hallowed trails of civilization, we require sources of purity. The space age requires pioneers who model what is needed. Religions that could provide this have been rocked to their foundations, but Celtic Christianity holds out the possibility of all these requirements.

In his *Brief Answers to the Big Questions*, Stephen Hawking concluded that our genes are too selfish to survive on this planet, that climate catastrophe and nuclear holocaust are likely, and that the future of homo sapiens lies in colonizing another planet and using science to rewrite our selfish genes. Religion is dismissed as a way of changing selfish genes because for much of its history it has become hostage to power politics and to corruption in its hierarchies.

Yet neither science nor secularism has eliminated faith—we have merely replaced faith in God with faith in an ism. We worship celebrity, money or tribe as fake substitutes for God. Tribes and kingdoms in the classical Celtic period had their power struggles and battles, but a grass-roots movement that crossed tribal boundaries declared ceaseless war on our selfish genes and sought to enthrone justice and mercy as the basis for common life.

It used to be said that materialism and science would cause religion to recede. Instead it has exploded worldwide. Religion formed the framework of freedom in Eastern Europe's discarding of communism and Iran's discarding of Western imperialism.

We now know through Darwin's successors that we humans share DNA with all creatures and elements of the cosmos. Some Christians retreat into medieval Bible constructs—God directly made humans, put us in control of the world and the rest is rubbish—or become atheists. Religion that denies science is a deadly thing. Celtic Christianity enables us to see God in every element and in every step of the human journey.

Our old understanding of natural and economic laws—that growth and consumption could go on forever and that hard work always pays off—no longer applies. Barbara Kingsolver charts the US breakdown in her novel *Unsheltered*.[199] There are two responses to this ending of the old world order—a hardening of mass denial and an opening to deeper realities. Celtic Christianity speaks to these deeper realities.

This Dark Age may consist of the replacement of liberal democracies by Big Brother dictatorships. It could be worse: mass destruction upon planet Earth and the migration of homo sapiens to other planets.

Whichever it is, homo sapiens will face the issue of the survival of the fittest. Are the fittest those with the strongest egos, or is the truth as Jesus said, that "the meek shall inherit the earth"?

The book of Revelation visualizes the ultimate community of the cosmos as the City of God with twelve foundations (Revelation 21:14) and twelve healing fruits (Revelation 22:2), led by twelve apostles (and their peoples) who have the keys to God's kingdom.

This book identifies twelve keys that can open doors in dark times, heal what is broken, and lay foundations for a new civilization of love:

1. Connect with Jesus as God at the heart of creation and care for it as he directs.
2. Let First, Second and Third Nation peoples (indigenous, rich and poor, black and white) journey together in the dignity of difference.
3. Embrace fresh expressions of "Roots, Rhythms, Reality and Relationships".
4. Weave together Christianity's God-given strands that have become separated—scriptural and sacramental, charismatic and communal.
5. Release the Divine Feminine/Masculine glory: Let women as well as men flow in their greatness
6. Invite the Spirit to speak to us through the varied constructs in Sacred Scriptures.
7. Draw living water from our spiritual well-springs.
8. Focus on what is deepest in us—God in the beauty of our origins.
9. Re-connect with the movements of Christ—freed from imperial hijackings—ever ancient, ever new.
10. Restore restitutional justice as the medicine for crime and social ailments.
11. Make our common global home in the eternal Communing of the Three Loves in God's heart.
12. Grow true community in our friendships, neighbourhoods and world.

"How dare you?" sixteen-year-old Greta Thunberg challenged the 2019 UN General Assembly in New York, in the presence of Donald Trump: "We are in the beginning of a mass extinction and all you can talk about is money and fairy tales of eternal economic growth." Celtic Christianity offers a way, in the face of catastrophes on earth, for humans to cherish creation and be directed by the Christ from whom creation emanates. It is universal and its greatest era lies ahead.

Select Bibliography

Allchin, A. M., *Praise Above All: Discovering the Welsh Tradition* (Cardiff: University of Wales Press, 1991).

Athanasius, *The Life of Antony* and *The Letter to Marcellinus*, trans. Robert C. Gregg (London: Kessinger Publishing, 2010).

Bede, *The Ecclesiastical History of the English People*, Oxford World's Classics (Oxford: Oxford University Press, 1999).

Berresford Ellis, Peter, *Celtic Women: Women in Celtic Society and Literature* (London: Constable, 1995).

Bieler, Ludwig, *The Irish Penitentials* (Dublin: Institute for Advanced Studies, 1975).

Bradley, Ian, *Following the Celtic Way: A New Assessment of Celtic Christianity* (London: Darton, Longman and Todd, 2018).

Bradley, Ian, *Celtic Christianity: Making Myths and Chasing Dreams* (Edinburgh: Edinburgh University Press, 1999).

Bradley, Ian, *Colonies of Heaven* (London: Darton, Longman and Todd, 2000).

Cassian, John, *Conferences*, trans. Colm Luibheid (New York: Paulist Press, 1985).

Cassian, John, *The Institutes*, trans. Boniface Ramsey (New York: Newman Press, 2000).

Charles-Edwards, T. M., *Early Christian Ireland* (Cambridge: Cambridge University Press, 2008).

Charles-Edwards, T. M., *The Chronicle of Ireland (Translated Texts for Historians)* (Liverpool: Liverpool University Press, 2006).

Clancy, Thomas, and Gilbert Markus, *Iona: The Earliest Poetry of a Celtic Monastery* (Edinburgh: Edinburgh University Press, 1995).

Connolly, Hugh, *The Irish Penitentials* (Dublin: Four Courts Press, 1995).

Davies, Oliver, *Celtic Christianity in Early Medieval Wales: The Origins of the Welsh Spiritual Tradition* (Cardiff: University of Wales Press, 1996).

Davies, Oliver (ed.), *Celtic Spirituality*, The Classics of Western Spirituality Series (New York: Paulist Press, 1999).

Davies, Wendy, "The Myth of the Celtic Church", in Nancy Edwards and Alan Lone (eds), *The Early Church in Wales and the West* (Oxford: Oxbow Books, 1992).

Evans, R. F., *Four Letters of Pelagius* (Eugene, OR: Wipf & Stock, 2010).

Fell, Christine, *Women in Anglo-Saxon England and the Impact of 1066* (London: British Museum Publications, 1984).

Ferguson, J., *Pelagius: A Historical and Theological Study* (Cambridge, 1956).

Flood, W. H. G., *History of Irish Music* (Dublin: Browne and Nolan, 1906).

Flower, Robin, *The Irish Tradition* (Oxford, 1947).

Gerald of Wales, *The Journey Through Wales and the Description of Wales* (London: Penguin, 1978).

Gougaud, Louis, *Christianity in Celtic Lands* (Dublin: Four Courts Press, 1992).

Graham, Hugh, *The Early Irish Monastic Schools* (Dublin: Talbot Press Ltd, 1923).

Haddan, A. W., and W. Stubbs, *Councils and Ecclesiastical Documents Relating to Great Britain and Ireland II* (Oxford: Oxford University Press, 1873).

Hahn-Hahn, Ida von, *The Fathers of the Desert, Volume 2* (London: Burns & Oates, 1907; reprinted by Forgotten Books, 2015).

Hollis, Stephanie, *Anglo-Saxon Women and the Church: Sharing a Common Fate* (Woodbridge: Boydell Press, 1992).

Joyce, P. W., *A Social History of Ireland*, 2 vols (Dublin, 1913).

Kenney, James F., *The Sources for the Early History of Ireland: Ecclesiastical* (Dublin: Four Courts Press, 1997).

Mackey, James P., *An Introduction to Celtic Christianity* (Edinburgh: T & T Clark, 1995).

Maidin, Uinseann O., *The Celtic Monk: Rules and Writings of Early Irish Monks* (Kalamazoo: Cistercian Publications, 1996).

Markus, Gilbert, "The End of Irish Christianity", Epworth Review 24 (1997), pp. 45-55.

Mayhew-Smith, Nick, *The Naked Hermit: A Journey to the Heart of Celtic Britain* (London: SPCK, 2019).

Meyer, Kuno, *Ancient Irish Poetry* (London: Constable, 1994).

Nicholson, M. Forthomme, "Celtic Theology: Pelagius", in James P. Mackey, ed., *An Introduction to Celtic Christianity* (Edinburgh: T & T Clark, 1995), pp. 386–413.

Nennius, *The History of the Britons* (London: Kessinger Publishing, 2004).

Ó Siodhacháin, Patricia Herron, "From Oral Tradition to Written Word: the History of Ancient Irish Law", *Studies: An Irish Quarterly Review*, 101/403 (2012), pp. 323–34 (Published by Irish Province of the Society of Jesus, <https://www.jstor.org/stable/23333152>).

Paor, Liam de, *Saint Patrick's World* (Dublin: Four Courts Press, 1993).

Rees, B. R., *Pelagius: A Reluctant Heretic* (Woodbridge: Boydell Press, 1988).

Reeves, William (ed.), *Life of St. Columba, founder of Hy, written by Adamnan* (Dublin: Irish Archaeological and Celtic Society, 1857).

Scott, Archibald, *The Pictish Nation: its people and its church* (Edinburgh & London: T. N. Foulis, 1918).

Severus, Sulpicius, "Life of Martin of tours", in Carolinne White (ed.), *Early Christian Lives* (London: Penguin, 1998).

Simpson, Ray, *Exploring Celtic Spirituality* (Stowmarket: KM Publishing, revised Study Guide edition, 2004).

Simpson, Ray, *Soulfriendship: Celtic Insights Into Spiritual Mentoring* (London: Hodder & Stoughton, 1999).

Simpson, Ray, *New Celtic Monasticism for Everyday People with Study Guide* (Slowmarket: KM Publishing, 2014).

Simpson, Ray, with Brent Lyons Lee, *St. Aidan's Way of Mission: Celtic insights for a post-Christian world* (Abingdon: BRF, 2016).

Simpson, Ray, and Brent Lyons Lee, *Celtic Spirituality in an Australian Landscape* (Lindisfarne: Saint Aidan Press, 2014).

Taylor, Thomas (ed.), *The Life of St Samson of Dol* (London: SPCK, 1925).

Todd, James Henthorn, *Leabhar Imuinn. The Book of Hymns of the Ancient Church of Ireland* (Dublin: Irish Archaeological and Celtic Society, 1855–69).

Warren, F. E., *The Liturgy and Ritual of the Celtic Church* (Woodbridge: Boydell Press, 1987).

Williams, Ifor (ed.), *The Poems of Taliesin*, trans. J. E. Caerwyn Williams, Mediaeval and Modern Welsh Series 3 (Dublin: Dublin Institute for Advanced Studies, 1987).

Wormald, Patrick, *The Times of Bede: Studies in Early English Christian Society and its Historian* (Oxford: Blackwell, 2006), includes appendix on 'Hilda, Saint and Scholar'.

Young, Simon, *The Celtic Revolution: In Search of 2000 Forgotten Years that Changed the World* (London: Gibson Square, 2009).

Notes

1.   Naomi Klein, *This Changes Everything* (London: Penguin, 2015).

2.   Gilbert Markus, "The End of Celtic Christianity", *Epworth Review* 24:3 (1997), p 45–55.

3.   Thomas Owen Clancy and Gilbert Markus, *Iona: The Earliest Poetry of a Celtic Monastery* (Edinburgh: Edinburgh University Press, 1995).

4.   Ian Bradley, *Following the Celtic Way: A New Assessment of Celtic Christianity* (London: Darton, Longman and Todd, 2018).

5.   K. H. Jackson, *Studies in Early Celtic Nature Poetry* (first published in 1936, Cambridge: Cambridge University Press, 2011); *A Celtic Miscellany* (first published in 1951, London: Penguin, 1971); Mary Low, *Celtic Christianity and Nature: Early Irish and Hebridean Traditions* (Edinburgh: Edinburgh University Press, 1997).

6.   Robert Van De Weyer, *The Letters of Pelagius: Celtic Soul Friend* (St Louis, MO: Turtleback Books, 1997).

7.   <https://celt.ucc.ie//published/L201054/index.html>.

8.   John Carey, *A Single Ray of the Sun: Religious Speculation in Early Ireland* (Aberystwyth: Centre for Advanced Welsh and Celtic Studies, 1999).

9.   *The Classics of Western Spirituality*, *Celtic Spirituality*, translated and introduced by Oliver Davies (Mahwah, NJ: Paulist Press, 1999), pp 49 and 327.

10.   See Helen Waddell, *Beasts and Saints* (London: Constable, 1934); Life, edited by Charles Plummer, is contained in *Vita Sancti Coemgeni* (Life of St Kevin) in *Vitae Sanctorum Hiberniae*, Vol. 1 (Oxford: Clarendon Press, 1910).

11.   Nick Mayhew-Smith, *The Naked Hermit: A Journey to the Heart of Celtic Britain* (London: SPCK, 2019).

12.   Robert Brown, "Exploring the Theology of the Bewcastle Cross: Then and Now", <http://www.academia.edu/1829958/Exploring_the_Theology_of_the_Bewcastle_Cross_Then_and_Now>.

[13] Rosemary Cramp and Richard N. Bailey, *Corpus of Anglo-Saxon Stone Sculpture: Cumberland, Westmorland and Lancashire North-of-the-Sands*, Vol. II, (London: The British Academy, 1988), p. 69.

[14] Michelle Brown, *The Lindisfarne Gospels: Society, Spirituality and the Scribe*, 1st edition (London: British Library Publishing, 2003), pp. 379 and 383.

[15] David Wallace-Wells, *The Uninhabitable Earth: A Story of the Future* (London: Allen Lane, 2019).

[16] J. Philip Newell, *Christ of the Celts* (Glasgow: Wild Goose Publications, 2009).

[17] David Adam, *Love the World* (London: SPCK, 2018).

[18] <https://www.st-columba.com/laying-spiritual-foundations-2017/>.

[19] Catherine Thom, *Early Irish Monasticism* (London: T & T Clark, 2007).

[20] Used with permission of Celtic Springs, Escomb.

[21] Benedicta Ward, *Give Love and Receive the Kingdom: Essential People and Themes of English Spirituality* (Brewster, MA: Paraclete Press, 2018), chapter 4.

[22] H. J. Massingham, *The Tree of Life* (London: Chapman & Hall, 1943).

[23] Black Elk's speech is widely quoted, for example in Dee Brown, *Bury My Heart at Wounded Knee: An Indian History of the American West* (New York: Vintage Books, 1987).

[24] Richard Twiss, *One Church Many Tribes: Following Jesus the Way God Made You* (Ventura, CA: Regal Books, 2010); *Rescuing the Gospel from the Cowboys: a native American expression of the Jesus Way* (Downers Grove: InterVarsity Press, 2015).

[25] Daniel N. Paul, *We Were Not the Savages: Collision Between European and Native American Civilizations* (First Nations History) (Black Point, Nova Scotia: Fernwood, 2006).

[26] <http://www.vatican.va/roman_curia/congregations/cfaith/cti_documents/rc_cti_1988_fede-inculturazione_en.html>.

[27] <https://w2.vatican.va/content/john-paul-ii/en/encyclicals/documents/hf_jp-ii_enc_07121990_redemptoris-missio.html>.

[28] The full text of the address can be found in Frank Brennan, *Reconciling Our Differences* (Melbourne: David Lovell, 1992), pp. 93–101.

[29] Letter to St Aidan Trust UK.

[30] Duncan Barrow, *Rethinking Celtic Art* (Oxford: Oxbow Books, 2008).

[31] Barry Cunliffe, *The Ancient Celts* (Oxford: Oxford University Press, 1997).

32   James Manco, *Blood of the Celts: The New Ancestral Story* (London: Thames and Hudson, 2015).

33   Simon Young, *The Celtic Revolution: In Search of 2000 Forgotten Years that Changed the World* (London: Gibson Square, 2009).

34   Lecture at Oxford University on 21 October 1955, in J. R. R. Tolkien, *The Monsters and the Critics, and Other Essays*, ed. Christopher Tolkien (London: Allen & Unwin, 1983).

35   From the introduction to Ray Simpson, *The Celtic Hymnbook* (Stowmarket: Kevin Mayhew, 2007).

36   Donald Meek, *The Quest for Celtic Christianity* (Haddington: Handsel Press, 2000), p. 120.

37   *The Classics of Western Spirituality, Celtic Spirituality*, translated and introduced by Oliver Davies (Mahwah, NY: Paulist Press, 1999).

38   Benedicta Ward, *High King of Heaven: Aspects of Early English Spirituality* (London: Continuum, 1999).

39   Paul Cavill, *Anglo-Saxon Christianity: Exploring the Earliest Roots of Christianity in England* (London: Fount, 1999).

40   Bede, *Ecclesiastical History of the English People*, edited with an introduction and notes by Judith McClure and Roger Collins (Oxford: Oxford University Press, 1999).

41   In personal conversation.

42   Ward, *High King of Heaven*, Preface.

43   Edmund Bishop, *Liturgica Historica: Papers on the Liturgy and Religious Life of the Western Church* (Oxford: Clarendon Press, 1917).

44   Bradley, *Following the Celtic Way*.

45   Ray Simpson, *New Celtic Monasticism for Everyday People* (KM Publishing, 2014), p. 36.

46   Basil Hume, *Footprints of the Northern Saints* (London: Darton, Longman and Todd, 1996).

47   John Macquarrie, *Paths in Spirituality* (London: SCM Press, 1972).

48   Ray Simpson, *Celtic Spirituality: Rhythm, Roots and Relationships* (Nottingham: Grove Books, 2003).

49   Ray Simpson and Brent Lyons Lee, *Celtic Spirituality in an Australian Landscape* (Lindisfarne: St Aidan Press, 2014), p 11.

50   Michito Kakutani, *The Death of Truth* (London: William Collins, 2018).

51 Wendy Davies, "The Myth of the Celtic Church", in Nancy Edwards and Alan Lane, eds, *The Early Church in Wales and the West* (Oxford: Oxbow Books, 1992, vol. 16).

52 Gilbert Markus, "The End of Celtic Christianity", *Epworth Review* 24 (1997), pp. 45–55.

53 Markus, "The End of Celtic Christianity", referring to *Liber Angeli* 29: <https://celt.ucc.ie//published/L201080/index.html>.

54 Bede, *Ecclesiastical History*, Chapter 2.

55 *Concilia, Decreta, Leges, Constitutiones in re Ecclesiarum Orbis Britannici*, vol. 2, Arthur Haddan and William Stubbs, eds, *Councils and Ecclesiastical Documents Relating to Great Britain and Ireland* (4 vols) (Oxford: Clarendon Press, 1869–78).

56 *Scriptores Latini Hiberniae*, vol. 5, *The Irish Penitentials*, edited by Ludwig Bieler (Dublin: The Dublin Institute for Advanced Studies, 1975).

57 Daphne Brooke, *Wild Men and Holy Places: St. Ninian, Whithorn and the Medieval Realm of Galloway* (Edinburgh: Canongate Press, 1994), p. 19.

58 James Kenney, *The Sources for the Early History of Ireland: an introduction and guide. Volume 1: Ecclesiastical* (Dublin: Four Courts Press, 1997), Chapter 3.

59 Lutz von Padberg, *Die Christianisierung Europas im Mittelalter*, Reclams Universal-Bibliothek (Leipzig: Reclam Verlag, 2009).

60 *Epistola* 76, PL 77: 1215–1216; From internet medieval sourcebook, <http://www.fordham.edu/Halsall/source/greg1-mellitus.txt>

61 St Columbanus, Letter 5, in *Sancti Columbani Opera*, in G. S. M. Walker, ed., *Scriptores Latini Hiberniae*, vol. 2 (Dublin Institute for Advanced Studies, 1957).

62 Roger Ellis and Chris Seaton, *The New Celts* (Milton Keynes: Kingsway, 1998), Chapter 2.

63 "*Ad Gentes Divinitus* [Decree on the Church's Missionary Activity]," in *Vatican Council II, Constitutions, Decrees, Declarations . . .* , gen. ed. Austin Flannery (New York, NY: Costello Publishing House; Dublin: Dominican Publications, 1996).

64 William Stubbs, Arthur West Haddan and David Wilkins, *Councils and Ecclesiastical Documents Relating to Great Britain and Ireland, Volume 2, part 2* (Oxford: Palala Press, reprint from Oxford University Press, 1878), Appendix B.4.

65   Michael Mitton, *Restoring the Woven Cord: Strands of Celtic Christianity for the Church today* (London: Darton, Longman & Todd, 1995).

66   Ray Simpson, *Church of the Isles: a prophetic strategy for the emerging church in Britain and Ireland* (Stowmarket: Kevin Mayhew, 2003), p. 231.

67   Maria Raikes, *Light from Dark Ages? An Evangelical Critique of Celtic Spirituality* (Cambridge: The Latimer Trust, 2012), p. 58.

68   Thomas Merton, *Conjectures of a Guilty Bystander* (New York: Doubleday, 1966), based on journal entry, April 1966.

69   Douglas Dales, Geoffrey Rowell and Rowan Williams (eds), *Glory Descending: Michael Ramsey & His Writings*, Canterbury Studies in Spiritual Theology (Norwich: Canterbury Press, 2005), Chapter 4.

70   Dales et al, eds, *Glory Descending*, Part One: 2.

71   Michelle P. Brown, *The Lindisfarne Gospels: Society, Spirituality and the Scribe* (London: British Library Publishing, 2003).

72   *Moluag: Patron of the Picts* by Fr Niall, <http://www.bachuilcountryhouse.co.uk/StMoluag.htm>.

73   From 1996 to 2006, *Ecotheology* published eleven volumes that are now archived and available at the website of JSRNC, <https://en.wikipedia.org/wiki/Journal_for_the_Study_of_Religion,_Nature_and_Culture>.

74   Markus, "The End of Celtic Christianity".

75   T. M. Charles-Edwards, *Early Christian Ireland* (Cambridge: University of Cambridge Press, 2008), pp. 224–6.

76   Colman Etchingham, *Church Organisation in Ireland* AD *650–1000* (Maynooth: Laigin Publications, 1999).

77   Charles Stewart, *The Gaelic Kingdom in Scotland, Its Origin and Church* (London: Simpkin, Marshall & Co., 1880).

78   Liam de Paor, *Saint Patrick's World* (Dublin: Four Courts Press, 1993).

79   Sean O Duinn OSB, *Where Three Streams Meet: Celtic Spirituality* (Dublin: The Columba Press, 2000).

80   Davies, *The Classics of Western Spirituality, Celtic Spirituality*, p. 122.

81   Oliver Davies, *Celtic Christianity in Early Medieval Wales* (Cardiff: University of Wales Press, 1996), p. 43.

82   Meg Llewellyn, *Celtic Miracles and Wonders: Tales of the Ancient Saints (Collected Volumes 1–6)* (Anamchara Books, 2015), p. 80.

83   Alice Curtayne, *St. Brigid of Ireland* (London: Sheed and Ward, 1954).

[84] Lisa M. Bitel, *Land of Women: Tales of Sex and Gender from Early Ireland* (Ithaca, NY: Cornell University Press, 1996).

[85] C. Plummer, ed., "Life of Ita", in *Vitae Sanctorum Hiberniae*, two vols (Dublin: Four Courts Press, 1997).

[86] David Rollason, Conrad Leyser and Hannah Williams, eds, *England and the Continent in the Tenth Century: Studies in Memory of Wilhelm Levison (1876–1947)* (Turnhout: Brepols, 2012).

[87] Christine Fell, *Women in Anglo-Saxon England and the impact of 1066* (London: British Museum Publications, 1984).

[88] Ray Simpson, *Hilda of Whitby: a spirituality of now* (Abingdon: BRF, 2014).

[89] Whitley Stokes, *The Martyrology of Oengus the Culdee* (repr. Dublin, 1984).

[90] Alexander Carmichael, *The Carmina Gadelica* Volume III, (Edinburgh: Oliver and Boyd, 1940), pp. 77–9.

[91] <https://www.christiandoctrine.com/christian-doctrine/other-religions-cults-and-sects/522-celti>.

[92] Ian Bradley, *Following the Celtic Way: A New Assessment of Celtic Christianity* (London: Darton, Longman and Todd, 2018).

[93] N. D. O'Donoghue, *The Mountain Behind the Mountain* (Edinburgh: T. and T. Clark, 1993), p. 38.

[94] *The Book of Lismore* 11: 4600–1; 1: 4602.

[95] Whitley Stokes and John Strachan, *Thesaurus Palaeohibernicus: A Collection of Old Irish Glosses* (Cambridge: Cambridge University Press, 1830-1909).

[96] David Cole, *The Mystic Path of Meditation: Beginning a Christ-Centred Journey* (Anamchara Books, 2016).

[97] Janet Craven, *Ireland's first book: what does it say today?* (Dublin: Linden, 2007).

[98] N. J. D. White, *Libri Sancti Patricii: The Latin Writings of St. Patrick,* in *Proceedings of the Royal Academy* (Dublin: Hodges Figgis & Co, 1905).

[99] James Henthorn Todd, *Leabhar Imuinn. The Book of Hymns of the Ancient Church of Ireland* (Dublin: Irish Archaeological and Celtic Society, 1855–69).

[100] Bede, *Ecclesiastical History of the English People* (Oxford: Oxford University Press, 1999), 3:5.

[101] Ron Ferguson, *George MacLeod: Founder of the Iona Community* (Glasgow: Wild Goose Publications, 2004).

[102] John Cassian, *Conferences*, trans. Colm Luibheid (New York: Paulist Press, 1985), 14.10.

[103] *The Life of St Samson of Dol*, ed. Thomas Taylor (Llanerch: Llanerch Press, 1991).

[104] <https://archive.org/stream/revueceltiqu20pari#page/30/mode/2up>.

[105] Leslie Hardinge, *The Celtic Church in Britain* (London: SPCK, 1972).

[106] Stokes and Strachan, *Thesaurus Palaeohibernicus: A Collection of Old-Irish Glosses*.

[107] Fergus Kelly, *A Guide to Early Irish Law*, Early Irish Law Series 3 (Dublin: Dublin Institute for Advanced Studies, 1988).

[108] <https://www.fourcourtspress.ie>.

[109] Jane Cartwright, ed., *Celtic Hagiography and Saints' Cults* (Cardiff: University of Wales Press, 2003), especially the contribution by Professor John T. Koch, Senior Fellow and Project Leader, Ancient Britain and the Atlantic Zone Project, and professor at the University of Wales Centre for Advanced Welsh and Celtic Studies.

[110] The Whithorn Trust, <https://www.whithorn.com>.

[111] University of Oxford, News and Events 14 February 2019.

[112] Ray Simpson, *Soulfriendship: Celtic insights into spiritual mentoring* (London: Hodder & Stoughton, 1999).

[113] See <https://www.pilgrimpath.ie/>.

[114] Miroslav Volf, *The End of Memory: Remembering Rightly in a Violent World* (Grand Rapids, MI: William B Eerdmans, 2006).

[115] Michael Ramsey, *Retreat Addresses given to the Oratory of the Good Shepherd*, Clewer, 1972, pp. 6–7, in Geoffrey Rowell, Kenneth Stevenson and Rowan Williams, eds, *Love's Redeeming Work: The Anglican Quest for Holiness* (Oxford: Oxford University Press, 2003).

[116] Theodore De Bruyn, *Pelagius's Commentary on St Paul's Epistle to the Romans*, Oxford Early Christian Studies (Oxford: Oxford University Press, 1997).

[117] Robert Van De Weyer (ed.), *The Letters of Pelagius: Celtic Soul Friend* (Little Gidding Books, 1996).

[118] Robert F. Evans, *Pelagius: Inquiries and Reappraisals* (Eugene, OR: Wipf and Stock, 2010).

[119] Markus, "The End of Celtic Christianity".

[120] E. A. Thompson, *Saint Germanus of Auxerre and the End of Roman Britain* (6), Studies in Celtic History (Woodbridge: Boydell Press, 1988).

[121] G. Bonner, "Pelagius (fl. c.390–418), theologian", *Oxford Dictionary of National Biography* (Oxford University Press, 2004).

[122] Bradley, *Following the Celtic Way*, p. 57.

[123] J. Philip Newell, *Christ of the Celts: The Healing of Creation* (Glasgow: Wild Goose Publications, 2008), p. 15.

[124] See for example, B. R. Rees, *Pelagius: A Reluctant Heretic* (Woodbridge: Boydell Press, 1988); *Pelagius: Life and Letters* (Martlesham: Boydell Press, 2004); *The Life of St. Morgan of Wales AKA Pelagius: A tract for the Anamchara Celtic Church* by The Revd Thomas J. Faulkenbury, <https://www.gospeltruth. net/stmorgan.htm>.

[125] Evans, *Pelagius: Inquiries and Reappraisals* (Eugene, OR: Wipf & Stock, 2010).

[126] Evans, *Pelagius: Inquiries and Reappraisals*, Chapter 5.

[127] Theodor De Bruyn, *Pelagius' Commentary on St Paul's Epistle to the Romans* (Oxford: Clarendon Press, 1993).

[128] The paragraphs above draw strongly from <https://www.academia. edu/26945227/Germanus_and_the_History_of_Pelagianism_in_Britain_ in_the_fifth_and_sixth_centuries>.

[129] David Cole, *Celtic Lent: 40 days of devotions to Easter* (Abingdon: BRF, 2018), p. 101.

[130] B. R. Rees, *Pelagius: Life and Letters* (Martlesham: Boydell Press, 2004), pp. 44–127).

[131] Philip Newell, *Listening to the heartbeat of God: A Celtic Spirituality* (London: SPCK, 2008), p. 127.

[132] Ian Bradley, *Celtic Christianity: Making Myths and Chasing Dreams* (Edinburgh: Edinburgh University Press, 1999), Introduction.

[133] A. O. Anderson, *Early Sources of Scottish History 500–1286, Vol. 2* (Stamford: Paul Watkins, 1990).

[134] N. Chadwick, *Studies in the British Church* (Cambridge: Cambridge University Press, 1958), p. 172.

[135] Terry Eagleton, *Crazy John and the Bishop and Other Essays on Irish Culture* (Cork: Cork University Press, 1998).

[136] Meg Llewellyn, *Celtic Miracles and Wonders: Tales of the Ancient Saints* (New York: Anamchara Books, 2017).

[137] Susan Power Bratton, *Christianity and the Irish Landscape in Lady Augusta Gregory's* A Book of Saints and Wonders, <http://www.baylorisr.org/ wp-content/uploads/bratton_irish.pdf>.

[138] <http://waymarksoflife.com/>.

[139] Rob Mackintosh, *The Rule of St Benedict, Nine Disciplines for Effective Leadership, an introduction* (printed by The Leadership Institute, 2002).

[140] Bradley, *Celtic Christianity*, p. ix.

[141] David Tacey, *Re-enchantment: The New Australian Spirituality* (Sydney: HarperCollins, 2000).

[142] Brent Lyons Lee and Ray Simpson, *Celtic Spirituality in an Australian Landscape* (St. Aidan Press, 2014).

[143] Stephen Hawking, *Brief Answers to the Big Questions* (London: John Murray, 2018).

[144] K. Lack, *The Eagle and the Dove: The Spirituality of the Celtic Columbanus* (London: Triangle, 2000), p. 73.

[145] J. McNeill, *Medieval Handbooks of Penance* (New York: Columbia University Press, 1990).

[146] James F. Kenney, *The Sources for the Early History of Ireland: Ecclesiastical* (Dublin: Four Courts Press, 1997).

[147] Ludwig Bieler, *The Irish Penitentials* (Dublin: Institute for Advanced Studies, 1975), p. 45.

[148] See *The Fathers of the Desert Vol. 2* by Ida von Hahn-Hahn, trans. Emily Bowden, (London: Burns and Oates, 1907, reprinted by Forgotten Books).

[149] See *Three Orders of the Saints of Ireland* in Liam de Paor, *Saint Patrick's World* (Dublin: Four Courts Press, 1993), p. 225.

[150] E. G. Bowen, *Settlements of the Celtic Saints in Wales* (Cardiff: University of Wales Press, 1954).

[151] Jacob G. Ghazarian, *The Mediterranean Legacy in Early Celtic Christianity: A Journey from Armenia to Ireland* (London: Bennett & Bloom, 2006). See also T. Olden, *The Church of Ireland: Its Eastern Origin* (London: W. Gardner, Darton & Co., 1895).

[152] O. Davies, *Celtic Christianity in Early Medieval Wales* (Cardiff: University of Wales Press, 1996), pp. 10f.

[153] Evagrius, *The Praktikos and Chapters on Prayer*, Cistercian Studies Series, vol. 4, trans. John Eudes Bamberger OCSO (Kalamazoo: Cistercian Publications, 1972).

[154] See *The Irish Penitentials*, ed. Ludwig Bieler (Dublin: Dublin Institute for Advanced Studies, 1975).

[155] <https://www.theway.org.uk/back/482Tanner.pdf>.

[156] Hugh Connolly, *The Irish Penitentials and their Significance for the Sacrament of Penance Today* (Dublin: Four Courts Press, 1995).

[157] A. W. Haddan and W. Stubbs, *Councils and Ecclesiastical Documents Relating to Great Britain and Ireland II, I* (Oxford: Oxford University Press, 1873), pp. 119–21.

[158] R. Fletcher, *The Conversion of Europe: From Paganism to Christianity, 371–1386 AD* (London: Fontana Press, 1998).

[159] James F. Kenney, *The Sources for the Early History of Ireland: Ecclesiastical* (Dublin: Four Courts Press, 1997).

[160] Anonymous *Life of Cuthbert.*

[161] Uinseann O. Maidin, *The Celtic Monk: Rules & Writings of Early Irish Monks* (Kalamazoo, MI: Cistercian Publications c/o Liturgical Press, 1996).

[162] Rowan Williams, *Silence and Honey Cakes* (Oxford: Lion Hudson, 2004).

[163] David Runcorn, *Silence: Gateway to God* (Cambridge: Grove Books, 2017).

[164] Wendy Davies, *Wales in the Early Middle Ages* (Leicester: Leicester University Press, 1982).

[165] Bede, *Ecclesiastical History of the English People* (Oxford: Oxford University Press, 1999), 3:3.

[166] Ray Simpson, *The Joy of Spiritual Fitness* (Stowmarket: Kevin Mayhew Publishing, 2010).

[167] *The Poems of Taliesin,* ed. Ifor Williams, trans. J. E. Caerwyn Williams, Mediaeval and Modern Welsh Series, 3 (Dublin: Dublin Institute for Advanced Studies, 1987).

[168] M. B. de Paor, *Patrick: The Pilgrim Apostle of Ireland* (London: HarperCollins 1998).

[169] *Tripartite Life* 1:69.

[170] R. J. Daniel, *"Ymborth yr Enaid", gyda rhagymadrodd a nodiadau,* Cardiff, 1995. English translation in *Celtic Spirituality: The Classics of Western Spirituality,* translated and introduced by Oliver Davies (Paulist Press, 1999).

[171] Davies, *Celtic Spirituality,* p. 144.

[172] Quoted from Thomas Owen Clancy and Gilbert Markus, *Iona: The Earliest Poetry of a Celtic Monastery* (Edinburgh: Edinburgh University Press.

[173] Esther De Waal, *The Celtic Way of Prayer: Recovering the Religious Imagination* (Norwich: Canterbury Press, 2010), p. 38.

[174]   Eleanor Hull, *The poem-book of Gael. Translations from Irish Gaelic poetry into English prose and verse* (London: Chatto and Windus, 1912). This claims this verse is of ninth-century origin.

[175]   Gerald of Wales, Giraldus Cambrensis, *The Journey Through Wales* and *The Description of Wales*, ed. Betty Radice, trans. L. Thorpe (Penguin Classics; reprint edition, 1978), pp. 1, 10, 18.

[176]   Martin Wallace, *The Celtic Resource Book* (London: Church House Publishing, 2009).

[177]   John Healy, *Insula Sanctorem et Doctorum, or Ireland's Ancient Schools and Scholars* (Dublin: Sealy, Bryers & Walker, 1893).

[178]   Hugh Graham, *The Early Irish Monastic Schools: A Study of Ireland's Contribution to Early Medieval Culture* (Dublin: Talbot Press, 1923, reprinted by Forgotten Books).

[179]   John Ryan, *Irish Monasticism: Origins and Early Development* (Dublin: Irish Academic Press, 1986).

[180]   Hugh Graham, *The Early Irish Monastic Schools* (Forgotten Books Classic Reprint).

[181]   Daphne Brooke, *Wild Men and Holy Places* (Edinburgh: Canongate Press, 1994).

[182]   Healy, *Insula Sanctorem et Doctorum*.

[183]   William Reeves, *Adamnan's Life of St. Columba* (with extensive notes, Dublin: Irish Archaeological and Celtic Society, 1857).

[184]   J. H. Bernard and Robert Atkinson, eds, *The Irish Liber Hymnorum*, 2 vols (London: Henry Bradshaw Society, 1898).

[185]   W. H. G. Flood, *History of Irish Music* (Dublin: Browne and Nolan, 1906; reprinted 1970).

[186]   See, for example, *Miadslechta* in *The Ancient Laws of Ireland*, iv (Dublin: published on behalf of H. M. Stationer's Office, 1887), pp. 363f.

[187]   Liam de Paor, *Saint Patrick's World* (Dublin: Four Courts Press, 1993), p. 282.

[188]   Bede, *Ecclesiastical History of the English People*, pp. 194–5.

[189]   Tomás Ó Carragáin, "Is there an archaeology of lay people at early Irish monasteries?", <https://journals.openedition.org/cem/13620> (*Bulletin du centre d'etudes medieval Agrandir Original*) (jpeg, 240k). See also <https://www.researchgate.net/profile/Cormac_Bourke/publication/280578677_The_Excavation_of_an_Early_Medieval_Crannog_at_Newtownlow_County_Westmeath/links/55bbbeb808ae9289a0957540/>

The-Excavation-of-an-Early-Medieval-Crannog-at-Newtownlow-County-Westmeath.pdf>.

190 "Clonfad: an industrious monastery", in P. Stevens and J. Channing, eds, *Settlement and community in the Fir Tulach kingdom* (Dublin: Wordwell), pp. 107–34.

191 T. M. Charles-Edwards, *Early Christian Ireland* (Cambridge: Cambridge University Press, 2008).

192 C. Etchingham, *Church Organisation in Ireland* AD *650–1000* (Maynooth: Laigin Publications, 1999).

193 P. Sheldrake, *Living Between Two Worlds: Place and Journey in Celtic Spirituality* (London: Darton, Longman & Todd, 1995), p. 39.

194 Simon Reed, *Ancient Ways for Modern Churches* (Abingdon: BRF, 2013).

195 Ray Simpson, *High Street Monasteries* (Stowmarket: Kevin Mayhew Publishing, 2009), p. 102, and available as a download on <http://www.raysimpson.org/userfiles/file/Village_of_God_KMpdf.pdf>.

196 <https://www.nytimes.com/2018/08/15/opinion/catholic-church-sex-abuse-pennsylvania.html>.

197 *The Tablet*, 18 August 2018.

198 James Hawes, *The Shortest History of Germany* (London: Old Street Publishing, 2018).

199 Barbara Kingsolver, *Unsheltered* (London: Faber and Faber, 2018).

Lightning Source UK Ltd.
Milton Keynes UK
UKHW020636160821
388940UK00010B/740